原型性和语际相似度对中国学习者英语空间介词in使用影响研究

A Study of the Effects of Prototypicality and Degree of Equivalence on Chinese EFL Learners' Use of IN

徐庆利　著

山东大学出版社

图书在版编目(CIP)数据

原型性和语际相似度对中国学习者英语空间介词in使用影响研究/徐庆利著.—济南:山东大学出版社,2019.12

ISBN 978-7-5607-5974-6

Ⅰ.①原… Ⅱ.①徐… Ⅲ.①英语—介词—研究 Ⅳ.①H314.2

中国版本图书馆CIP数据核字(2020)第001077号

策划编辑:王　潇
责任编辑:王　潇
封面设计:张　荔

出版发行:山东大学出版社
社　址　山东省济南市山大南路20号
邮　编　250100
电　话　市场部(0531)88363008
经　销:新华书店
印　刷:山东和平商务有限公司
规　格:720毫米×1000毫米　1/16
11.5印张　213千字
版　次:2019年12月第1版
印　次:2019年12月第1次印刷
定　价:28.00元

前　言

本书是在本人的博士论文《原型性和语际相似度对中国英语学习者in使用影响研究——概念迁移视角》基础上撰写而成的，全书用英语完成，共分七章。本研究以英语空间介词 *in* 为例，旨在从中国学习者对英语名词概念指向识解的角度对影响空间介词习得的认知因素进行探讨，揭示学习者英语空间介词习得中概念迁移发生的机制。

本研究首先在认知语法和联结主义框架内论证了二语学习者英语空间介词 *in* 的使用依赖于学习者对名词指向的参照物范畴的识解，即 *in* 指向的图式化的容器能否得到名词指向的参照物概念的阐释。对于英语本族语者来说，阐释距离的远近取决于在母语习得过程中形成的对容器范畴原型性的判断。而对于二语学习者来说，则会受到容器范畴原型性和容器范畴语际异同两个因素的制约。

为验证此观点，本研究构建了容器范畴原型性和容器范畴语际异同分类框架。首先，基于相关文献，研究者依据英语空间介词 *in* 的各种用法，将英语中被识解为容器的参照物按照原型性逐渐递减的顺序分成七类。其次，研究者采用基于语料库的方法，对比分析英语名词与其汉语对等词参照物概念表征异同，按照完全对等、部分对等和零对等的顺序将英汉容器范畴相似度划分为六个等级。

在此基础上，本研究分别就容器范畴原型性和容器范畴语际相似度对中国学习者空间介词 *in* 使用的影响进行了实证研究。学习者语料通过看图填介词获取，介词测试卷依据上述两个分类设计。确定迁移发生的语料主要是通过四种对比以及对部分学习者的回顾性访谈获得。受试由三组不同英语水平的 150 名中国学习者组成，每组 50 人。具体研究问题如下：(1)范畴原型性怎样影响英语空间介词 *in* 的使用？(2)范畴原型性影响效应怎样随着学习者英语语言水平的变化而变化？(3)英汉容器范畴语际相似度怎样影响英语空间介词 *in* 的使用？(4)容器范畴语际相似度的影响效应怎样随着学习者语言水平的变化而变化？

研究结果表明：(1)范畴原型性和范畴语际相似度都会对 *in* 的使用产生影响。但不同原型性环境以及不同语际相似度下 *in* 的使用变化趋势表明，范畴语际相似度对学习者空间介词 *in* 的使用影响更显著。语际相似度越高，母语的正迁移效应越高，随着语际相似度的逐渐减弱，学习者 *in* 的使用越来越受到母语容器范畴的干扰。(2)在范畴原型性和范畴化语际相似度这两个因素影响效应的变化上，容器范畴原型性的影响效应随着二语水平的提高得到增强，但主要表现在高水平组，且其影响受制于范畴语际相似度，因为只有当各原型性环境语际相似度较一致时，高水平组 *in* 的使用才呈现出随着范畴原型性增强而逐步增多的线性趋势。对于范畴语际相似度来说，*in* 使用在水平组间的变化趋势表明随着语言水平的提高，语际相似的正迁移效应逐步增强，而语际差异引起的负迁移则逐步减弱。但研究也发现，虽然高水平组在各种语际类型环境中 *in* 的使用都高于其他水平组，但在语际差异程度较高时，*in* 的使用也因为母语容器范畴干扰出现显著性降低。

本研究首次揭示了范畴语际相似度是空间介词 *in* 使用中迁移发生的概念机制，同时也表明了学习者对名词空间概念的识解在介词使用中的重要作用，这对研究其他关系类语义结构习得中的认知机制具有重要的启示，同时对英语教学也具有重要的实践价值。

本研究顺利完成首先要感谢我的导师刘振前教授。四年求学期间，老师严谨治学的态度、一丝不苟的作风使我对学习始终不敢有丝毫懈怠；论文写作期间，老师不断询问、督促论文进展，多次要求进行论文工作汇报，同时在写作遇到困难时及时给予鼓励和指导。感谢老师的耐心、细心和苦心。

我要感谢山东大学王俊菊教授、马文教授、王湘云教授，同济大学张德禄教授，河南大学张克定教授，南京师范大学张辉教授，华南理工大学蔡金亭教授，曲阜师范大学鞠玉梅教授、秦洪武教授、王广成教授，感谢他们从选题到答辩给予我的悉心指导和精心点拨，帮助我一次次在迷茫和困境中找到新的研究思路。

我要感谢诸多学友在求学期间给予我的各种支持和鼓励。他们是共同度过四年博士生活的洪杰、朱海峰、程瑞兰、孙庆舒等，在工作和生活上帮助我解压的梁文花老师、寻阳老师、王秀卿老师、彭芳老师、鲁艳芳老师、张琳老师、王丽老师、孔蕾老师等。我要感谢我的家人，感谢他们对我的宽容和理解。他们始终如一的支持是我在求学道路上不断前进的重要动力。

本书能够出版得益于山东省社会科学规划研究项目“中国学习者英语空间介词 over 产出中母语迁移机制研究——认知语法视角(16CWZJ05)”的资助。最后感谢山东大学出版社为本书出版给予的大力支持。

作 者

2019 年 9 月

List of Figures

List of Tables

List of Abbreviations

A	Autonomous Structure
ACTL	Actual *le*
ANOVA	Analysis of Variance
BNC	British National Corpus
CCLC	Peking University-Center for Chinese Linguistics-Corpus
CL	Classifier
CTH	Conceptual Transfer Hypothesis
CLEC	Chinese Learner English Corpus
D	Dependent Structure
De_1	NP modification marker-*de*
De_2	VP modification marker-*de*
DUR	Durative-*zhe*
EXP	Experiential-*guo*
F	F Value
GCEPC	General Chinese-English Parallel Corpus
HG	High Group
IG	Intermediate Group
LG	Low Group
L1	First Language
L2	Second Language
LRH	Linguistic Relativity Hypothesis
MD	Mean Difference
MHM	Modified Hierarchical Model
RHM	Revised Hierarchical Model
p/sig.	Significance Probability
SPSS	Statistical Product and Service Solutions/Statistical Package of Social Studies

Contents

Chapter One Introduction

Whenever a spatial relation between two or two groups of objects is described, what initially occurs in one's mind is the category of the region delimited by the reference object for the located one. Is the region categorized as a container, a supporting surface or a path? Such a mental activity is argued to be a powerful determinant of senses ascribed to English spatial prepositions (Langacker 1987) and thereby constitutes the conceptual basis of the use of spatial prepositions. In second language (L2) acquisition research, first language (L1) transfer has always been reported to exert important influence on learners' use of English spatial prepositions (Correa-Beningfield 1985; Ijaz 1986; Ma 2007; Xu, et al. 2014; Zhang & Liu 2013). But the cognitive mechanism underlying L1 transfer is under-explored. This study, based on the conceptual dependence of the use of prepositions on the categorization of reference objects, is intended to investigate the conceptual mechanism of L1 transfer in the use of English spatial prepositions by Chinese learners of English as a foreign language.

1.1 Research Background

In English, spatial prepositions refer to a class of words which usually precede nouns or pronouns and which are used to indicate the spatial relation between the located object and the reference object (Lindstromberg 1997; Quirk, et al. 1998). While the number of prepositions is small in comparison with other lexical categories, prepositions have long been recognized as a big challenge to learners of English as a second language and remain problematic even for the advanced learners (Ijaz 1986; Ma 2007). Learners are always found to erroneously expand or narrow the semantic categories of prepositions (Jarvis & Pavlenko 2008; Odlin 2008), as can be easily seen in the following misuses taken from Chinese Learner English Corpus (CLEC) (Gui & Yang 2003):

(1) With the rug there are many holes on it.

(2) They play on the street with all kinds of colorful lanterns.

(3) The fried towel gourd is placed in a rounded and laced plate.

(4) We can read, write and so on under the light.

(5) Thróugh the fluorescent screen, I saw our Chinese athletes.

There seems to be much confusion among the learners about the semantic distinctions between the spatial preposition *in* and other spatial prepositions. For instance, in Example (1) the semantic category of the preposition *on* is expanded into that of the preposition *in*, whereas in Example (3), the semantic category of *in* is expanded into that of *on*. This confusion is partly attributed to the interference of L1 with language specificity in spatial semantic categories, thus, L1 transfer is one of the biggest concerns in studies of acquisition of English spatial prepositions by L2 learners.

While emphasis was placed in earlier studies on the identification of cases of L1 transfer to confirm or disconfirm the role of L1 in the acquisition of spatial prepositions of English as a L2 (Gui 2005; Khampang 1974; Mougeon, et al. 1979; Schumann 1986), focus since the mid 1980s has been shifted to the explanation of the process of L1 transfer, or, in other words, how L1 transfer occurs. Central to the explanation were the cognitive underpinnings of transfer in terms of cross-linguistic convergence and divergence in spatial categorization (Becker & Carroll 1997; Correa-Beningfield 1985; Ijaz 1986; Jarvis & Odlin 2000; Li & Cai 2008; Ma 2007; Xu, et al. 2014; Zhang & Liu 2013), which has been claimed to underlie the comprehension and production of spatial prepositions (Langacker 1987; Taylor 2002; Tyler & Evans 2003).

In these studies, two research paradigms can be identified. For the first one (Correa-Beningfield 1985; Ijaz 1986; Young-Davy 2000; Ma 2007), concepts tended to be equated with semantics of spatial prepositions and L1 transfer is attributed to the similarities and differences in semantic structures between English spatial prepositions and their translation equivalents. But recent developments in conceptual transfer research have propelled the studies to go beyond the semantic level and into the conceptual level. Attempts have been made to visualize the conceptual representations of prepositions in terms of perceptual experience or schemas (Becker & Carroll 1997; Jarvis & Odlin 2000; Xu, et al. 2014; Zhang & Liu 2013).

Both of the approaches to spatial categorization, though providing important insights into the cognitive mechanism of L1 transfer in the use of English spatial prepositions by L2 learners, are problematic in that little attention has been paid to the fact that spatial categorization as a mental process of identifying and classifying spatial relations between the objects is simply impossible without the categorization of objects in the first place (Langacker 1987; Aurnague, et al. 2007: 1-3). As Langacker (1987: 215) claimed, construal of a spatial relation is conceptually dependent on the categorization of objects involved in the spatial relation; "one cannot conceptualize interconnections without also conceptualizing the objects they interconnect". Talmy (2000: 182) also pointed out that "spatial characterizations expressed overtly ultimately rest on certain unexpressed spatial understandings".

(6) We were in the meadow opposite the Grotto.

(7) In the morning we sat opposite the Grotto, on the meadow.

(8) I stepped out of my chariot to walk across the meadow.

(9) The whole village marched through the meadow and up the hill to Polly's house. (BNC)①

In Examples (6)-(9) taken from British National Corpus (BNC), the use of four different prepositions before the noun *meadow* indicates the object meadow is construed as a container, a supporting surface, a surface serving as a path and a container serving as a path respectively. In other words, the varied spatial understandings of the same object lead to the activation of different semantic features and result in the production of different prepositions.

---

① The British National Corpus (BNC) is a 100 million word collection of samples of written and spoken language from a wide range of sources, designed to represent a wide cross-section of British English from the later part of the 20th century, both spoken and written. It was originally created by Oxford University Press in the 1980s-early 1990s.

Given the role played by the reference objects in the spatial relations, categories of reference objects are generally assumed to play a greater part in motivating the use of spatial prepositions. This was well illustrated in Hottenroth's (1993: 179) and Cuyckens' (1993: 37) claims that the semantic features of a preposition cannot be described without recourse to the reference objects. Taylor (2002: 234) also argued that a preposition "often imposes tighter restrictions on the semantic character of its landmark than its trajectory". All these arguments suggest a closer semantic relationship between the reference objects and prepositions.

(10) There is an apple ________ the plate.

In Example (10), which preposition, *in* or *on*, will be activated to combine with the noun *plate* is largely determined by how the plate is categorized. If it is construed as a container, *in* will be activated, whereas if it is construed as a supporting surface, *on* will be produced. It follows that what underlies the use of spatial prepositions is the categories of reference objects rather than the semantic or conceptual representations of prepositions. Therefore, any claim about the cognitive underpinnings of the use of spatial prepositions should be made on the basis of the investigation of what are involved in the categories of reference objects.

Within the framework of prototype theory (Lakoff 1987; Rosch 1978; Ungerer & Schmid 2001), categorization of objects involves in the first place an establishment of the prototypicality of members through a mental comparison between a given object and the category prototype (Langacker 1987: 371). Compare the three reference objects in the following spatial scenes:

(11) water in the bowl

(12) a nail in the wall

(13) a man in the line

The bowl, being three-dimensional, partially close, hollow and bounded, bears the greatest resemblance to the prototype of the CONTAINER category and is of the strongest prototypicality. The wall is farther from the prototype with the absence of the attribute "hollowness", and the one-dimensional line is on the boundary of the category with little resemblance to the prototype. The rise in the degree of prototypicality will increase the possibility for an object to be construed as a container and this will in turn lead to a high frequency of the combination between the preposition *in* and the noun referring to the object. To put it another way, the prototypicality of reference objects might be an important cognitive factor underlying the use of spatial prepositions by English natives. However, viewed from an interlingual perspective, things could get more complex (Ungerer & Schmid 2001: 50) because of the cross-linguistic differences in conceptual representations between L2 learners and natives. As claimed in connectionist approach to bilingual research, bilingual conceptual structure is a compound comprising both L1-based and L2-based categorization (Pavlenko 2009: 146). Thus, it might be reasonably assumed that categorization of reference objects is not only influenced by the prototypicality of objects established in the course of L2 acquisition but also by how well the two languages converge in categorization. Take the categorization of the two objects, the wall and the line, as an example. As mentioned above, the wall is more prototypical than the line as instances of the CONTAINER category, but as to the equivalence in categorization between English and Chinese, there tends to be zero equivalence in categorizing the wall but full equivalence in categorizing the line. This indicates that language distance does not always correspond with the prototypicality of reference objects, or in other words, strong prototypicality does not entail high degree of cross-linguistic equivalence in categorization. Then for a Chinese learner of English, how does he categorize the wall or the line? To put it another way, how does he construe the conceptual contents of the nouns (Langacker 2008: 55)? Is the construal more likely to be influenced by the prototypicality of the reference object or the degree of equivalence in categorization? Is the use of prepositions affected by his construal? Apparently, the exploration of these questions is contributory to revealing the cognitive basis of the use of *in* by L2 learners and to providing a cognitive account for L1 transfer in acquisition of spatial prepositions. For instance, as to the misuse of the preposition *on* in Example (1), a comparison of categorization of the object rug between English and Chinese shows that the misuse of *on* is due to learners' construal of *rug* as a supporting surface under the influence of L1-based categorization. This suggests that what is carried over to English is not the semantic or conceptual representation of *shang* but the conceptual representation of *di tan*.

To address the above issues, the study, taking the English spatial preposition *in* as an example, is intended to empirically investigate the effects of prototypicality of containers and the degree of equivalence in categorizing objects as containers on the use of *in* by Chinese EFL (English Foreign Language) learners to uncover the conceptual mechanism of L1 transfer. Such a conceptual approach to transfer also motivates the investigation of how transfer happens in acquisition of other relational predicates (e. g. , verbs, adjective or adverbs).

1.2 Objectives of the Study

The study serves several purposes. Firstly, the study is intended to demonstrate that the transfer in the use of the English spatial preposition *in* is facilitated or inhibited by learners' construal of containers, or, in Langacker's words, by learners' construal of the conceptual contents (Langacker 2008: 55) of nouns following the preposition *in*. In preposition learning and teaching, focus is always set on the semantic or conceptual representations of the prepositions to the exclusion of the conceptual representations of nouns collocating with prepositions. Actually many misuses of *in* are caused by the projection of the L1-specific CONTAINER category onto an English noun through the mediation of its Chinese equivalent. Therefore, an empirical investigation of the effects of categorization to reveal the conceptual mechanism of transfer in the use of *in* has important implications for English teaching.

Secondly, the study is aimed to highlight the importance of comparative studies in English teaching and learning. Transfer is claimed to be driven by learners' perceived similarity between L1 and L2 (Kellerman 1995: 131), on the basis of which learners selectively capitalize on L1 knowledge that they assume to be most relevant to L2 (Kellerman 1995: 130; Ringbom 1986: 150). As a result, an improper judgment of cross-linguistic similarities not only facilitates negative transfer from L1, but also inhibits positive transfer from L1. In this study, the effect of degrees of equivalence on the use of *in* by learners at different levels of L2 proficiency is testified and a continuum of cross-linguistic equivalence in the CONTAINER category is established on the basis of a corpus-based comparison between English and Chinese. All these will guide teachers to make comparisons in teaching to help learners form a proper judgment of cross-linguistic similarities.

The third objective of the study is to establish an analytical model accounting for the formation of a composite preposition structure [IN+N] by L2 learners within the framework of cognitive grammar and connectionist approach to bilingual conceptual representation. Much effort has been made by Niu (2008a, 2008b, 2011a, 2011b) to explain the mechanism underlying grammatical constructions in Chinese within the Analytic Model of Autonomy-dependency Alignment, but no attention has been paid to learner language. Focusing on learner language will provide interlanguage evidence for valence relation theory (Langacker 1987) and enhance the explanatory power of the Analytic Model of Autonomy-dependency Alignment. As to the bilingual research, the empirical study of the effect of the prototypicality of containers on learners' use of *in* will provide support to the interrelated nature of bilingual conceptual representation. In addition, the revelation of conceptual dependency of *in* on the nouns will also encourage researchers to think how to capture bilingual learners' processing of the relational predicates like *in*.

1.3 Organization of the Book

This book consists of seven chapters.

Chapter One is the introduction to the book, consisting of three parts: The research background, objectives of the study and the organization of the book.

Chapter Two starts with an analysis of what categories of reference objects involve within the framework of prototype theory. Then, a detailed review of relevant studies that have been previously conducted on conceptual transfer and acquisition of spatial prepositions by L2 learners is presented, on the basis of which the gaps in current studies are pointed out in an attempt to justify the proposed research project.

Chapter Three provides the theoretical basis on which the study of the effects of prototypicality and degrees of cross-linguistic equivalence in categorization on EFL learners' use of *in* is done. It firstly demonstrates the conceptual dependency of the use of the spatial preposition *in* on the CONTAINER category within the framework of cognitive grammar, and then discusses the involvement of two systems of categorization in the use of *in* by EFL learners on the basis of connectionist approach to bilingual conceptual representation.

Chapter Four presents a preliminary study of English-based prototype concept of CONTAINER and degrees of cross-linguistic equivalence in the CONTAINER category between English and Chinese. In this study, a continuum of prototypicality of containers and a continuum of degree of cross-linguistic equivalence in categorization of containers are proposed.

Chapter Five introduces the methodological framework of an empirical study on the hypothesized impacts of prototypicality and degrees of cross-linguistic equivalence on the use of the English spatial preposition *in* by Chinese-speaking learners.

Chapter Six reports and discusses the results of the study with respect to the research questions, through which degrees of equivalence as the conceptual mechanism of L1 transfer are empirically justified.

Chapter Seven firstly summarizes the major findings, then discusses the theoretical, methodological and pedagogical implications, and finally points out the limitations of the research and the directions for future research.

Chapter Two　Literature Review

2.1　Introduction

This chapter mainly consists of three parts. In the first part, a prototype approach to the categories of reference objects is proposed within the framework of prototype theory. Included in the second part is the introduction of the theoretical advances contributing to the development of conceptual transfer studies, a comprehensive definition of conceptual transfer and an overview of the achievements that have been made in conceptual transfer studies. The third part deals with a critical review of the empirical studies that have been done on the acquisition of spatial prepositions by L2 learners.

2.2　Categories of Reference Objects

As noted in Section 1. 1, categories of reference objects are argued to underpin the use of spatial prepositions. Therefore, an analysis of what categories of reference objects involve is required for the claims related to the cognitive basis of the use of spatial prepositions. In this section, the basic principles and assumptions of prototype theory are initially introduced; and then, a prototype approach to the categories of reference objects is proposed.

2.2.1　Prototype Theory

In this section, an introduction of prototype theory will be made from the following two aspects: Two principles of formation of categories and the basic assumptions held by prototype theory.

As cognitive linguists (Lakoff 1987, Landau & Jackendoff 1993, Ungerer & Schmid 2001) claimed, categories are stored in the mind as concepts and are the products of categorization which is the mental process of recognition and classification of things in the world (Ungerer & Schmid 2001). As an important cognitive faculty which enables us to "cut up the environment into classifications by which non-identical stimuli can be treated as equivalent" (Rosch, et al. 1976: 383), the nature of categorization has long been a concern since the time of Aristotle (Lakoff 1987). In the late 1960s and 1970s, a series of empirical studies (Berlin & Kay 1969; Kay & McDaniel 1978; Labov 1973; Rosch 1973, 1975, cited in Lakoff 1987) on the categorization of colors and vessels by human beings revealed that there tend to be a best example with respect to which things are put inside or outside the category. Rosch named the best example as prototype and generalized the above empirical proof into a new theoretical account of category, called "prototype theory" (Lakoff 1987; Ungerer & Schmid 2001: 10). To justify the prototype approach to categorization, two cognitive principles underlying the formation of categories were proposed by Rosch (1978).

2.2.1.1 Two Principles of Categorization

In accordance with Rosch (1978: 28), there are "two cognitive principles underlying the formation of categories: Cognitive economy and perceived world structure". The principle of cognitive economy was proposed to explain the purpose of human categorization by stating that "the task of category systems is to provide maximum information with the least cognitive effort" (Rosch 1978: 28). As Sperber and Wilson (2001: 46) claimed, human cognition tends to be organized so as to maximize cognitive efficiency and minimize the cost of cognitive resources. Simply put, human knowledge of the world is structured in the way that in face of a stimulus, one can retrieve from it maximum information relevant while conserving finite resources as many as possible. Categorization by prototypes is just such an efficient pattern of knowledge organization (Lakoff 1987; Rosch 1978). By centering around the most representative case of the category, categorization, on the one hand, "reduces the infinite differences among stimuli to behaviorally and cognitively usable proportions" (Rosch 1978: 29) whereby the stimuli are subsumed under the same category, on the other hand, it preserves the most relevant defining attributes to differentiate the stimuli in one category from those in the other category. As a result, while the objects shown in Figure 2. 1 are different in shapes and sizes, human beings have no difficulty in recognizing them as glasses used for holding liquid by focusing on the defining attributes that are shared by the containers (e. g. , material, hollowness and concavity) to the neglect of their differences in the non-defining attributes (e. g. , shape and size).

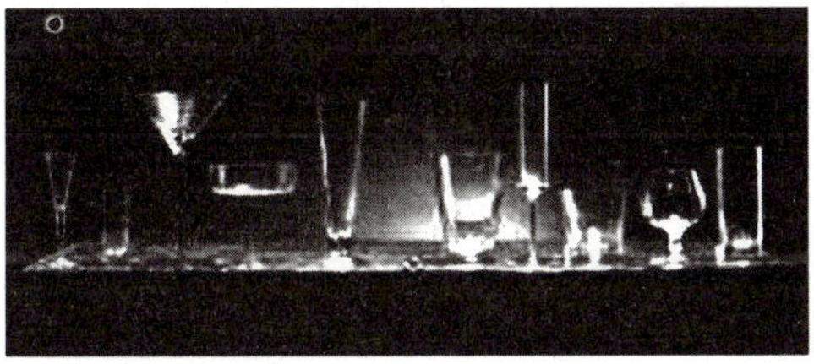

Figure 2. 1 Glasses in Different Shapes and Sizes (from http: //image. google. com)

The second principle "perceived world structure" is concerned with the internal structure of the economy-oriented category. The principle means that "unlike the sets of stimuli used in traditional laboratory concept attainment tasks, the perceived world is not an unstructured total set of equiprobable co-occurring attributes" (Rosch 1978: 29), but a structured network of highly correlated attributes as a result of the economy-directed cognitive processing. As shown in Figure 2. 1, the objects out there in the objective world are different in height, width or concavity depth. However, as they are picked up to hold the wine or water, they are perceived in such a way that only the attributes that are highly related to the functional need enter the minds of speakers coherently, for example, "curving inward", "being hollow inside" and "materially bounded on two sides". Here is one more example. A man wants to take a seat and yet there is no chair but a desk and a cat in the room. In this case, the geometrical attribute "having a surface" and the functional attribute "a surface to sit on" will be more likely to be activated together in the perceived structure of the desk than the cat, though the attribute "a surface to sit on" is not a defining one for either of the two categories. It, then, follows that the sensory and functional needs of the persons interacting with the immediate physical and social environment determine what attributes of the objects are highlighted to define the category. In other words, the formation of categories is grounded in our physiological and social experience during our interaction with the objective world (Tyler & Evans 2003).

2.2.1.2 Assumptions about Categorization Held by Prototype Theory

On the basis of the above two principles, prototype theory, standing in opposition to the classical approach, claims that categories are formed around prototypes which function as reference points to characterize other members (Rosch 1978, Lakoff 1987; Ungerer & Schmid 2001: 10). According to Taylor (2002: 59), the prototype might exist in two forms: (1) It can be treated as a specific member that is best representative of the category; (2) It can be referred to as a schematic representation of the conceptual core of the category. The two forms are closely related in that the former is the instantiation of the latter.

A series of specific assumptions about categorization have been proposed within the framework of prototype theory, which can be summarized in the following four aspects.

Firstly, category membership is not a matter of all or nothing, but rather it involves different degrees of typicality (Ungerer & Schmid 2001: 39). The typical member best exemplifies the category as a whole by sharing the maximum attributes with other category members and minimum attributes with members of contrasting categories (Ungerer & Schmid 2001: 29). Other members may belong to the category to varying degrees depending on their similarity to the prototype. The more similar the member is to the prototype, the more central its status is within the category (Taylor 2002: 60).

Secondly, family resemblance is an important principle governing the formation of category prototypes and the gradient of category membership (Ungerer & Schmid 2001: 2). As Rosch and Mervis (1975: 575) defined, the principle of family resemblance means that within a category each member shares at least one or more than one feature with one or more other members. In line with the principle, the members of a category are connected not because of "their identity" by sharing a single set of defining features but because of "their mutual similarity" by sharing different sets of features (Cuyckens 1993: 56). For instance, in the PLATE category, "having a flat surface" is normally considered an attribute "most distributed among the category members" (Rosch & Mervis 1975: 575). However, it is not a must to all members. As illustrated in Figure 2. 2, the PLATE category is extended by the family resemblance established between (a) and (b) and (b) and (c). To be precise, (b) is related with (a) by the attribute "concavity" and (c) is related with (b) by the attribute "shallowness".

(a) (b) (c)

Figure 2. 2 Members of the PLATE Category (from http://image.baidu.com)

This implies that the attributes contributing to the internal structure of the category are not necessarily "category-wide" (Ungerer & Schmid 2001: 26). The prototypical members of categories tend to be those who have most resemblance to other members of the category and least resemblance to the contrasting categories (Ungerer & Schmid 2001: 29).

Thirdly, there are several basic cognitive principles that contribute to the establishment of family resemblance between category members. The most important might be the principle of Gestalt perception (Hottenroth 1993; Ungerer & Schmid 2001), which can be generalized as: The parts of an object that are closely associated with the perceptual demands of viewers are perceived as an integral whole on the basis of mental proximity, similarity, closure and continuation (Ungerer & Schmid 2001: 34). In Figure 2. 3, the bowl is not materially bounded on all sides and does not locate the pear inside the materially delimited boundaries. Yet it is still construed as a container by means of mental closure of the material boundaries (Hottenroth 1993: 208). Such mental operation establishes the resemblance between the bowl and the category prototype.

Another important principle that is related to the effect of family resemblance is conceptual projection across domains realized by mapping the conceptualization of one category onto another (Hottenroth 1993: 209-210). For example, in the expression "there is a break in the line", the one-dimensional object is categorized as a container by means of the projection of a three-dimensional configuration onto one dimension (Hottenroth 1993: 210).

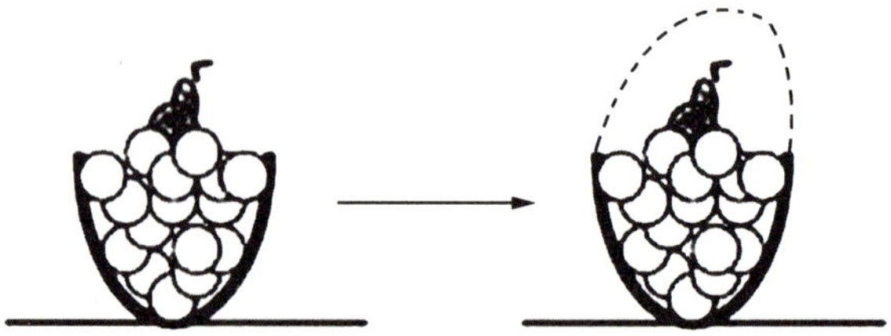

Figure 2.3 Mental Closure of the Bowl (Adapted from Garrod, et al. 1999: 168)

Characterization of objects in terms of topological properties also figures much in the realization of family resemblance. Topological characterization is mainly featured with magnitude neutrality and shape neutrality (Talmy 2000: 25-27, 187). Magnitude neutrality means that the categorization of objects in some cases has little bearing on the size of the objects. It is illustrated in Examples (14)-(17).

(14) She moved across the carpet.

(15) She moved across the room.

(16) The focus moved across the Atlantic to central Europe.

(17) Two heavy bombers moved across the sky. (BNC)

While the reference objects denoted by the nouns vary greatly in size, all are construed as a path that goes perpendicularly from one to the other of two parallel lines (Talmy 2000: 26). In the same vein, it can be observed from Examples (18)-(20) that the categorization of objects as "a path within a medium" is also indifferent to particulars of the shape (Talmy 2000: 27).

(18) He walked through the door.

(19) He walked through the lobby.

(20) He walked through the crowd. (BNC)

These mental manipulations of object concepts are largely functionally-motivated (Hottenroth 1993). Similar functional experience in interactions with the objects motivates human beings to focus on the aspects that are relevant to the particular purpose and to reduce the abundant information of the objects to one geometrical configuration by way of the above cognitive operations.

Fourthly, categorization is a personal and subjective mental activity, heavily influenced by the culture where a person grows up and lives (Ungerer & Schmid 2001: 50). Immersed in a culture where the campus is conventionally delimited by high walls in all directions and exposed to the expressions like *xiao yuan li* or *yuan zi li* since childhood, native Chinese speakers tend to put the object campus into the CONTAINER category. However, for native English speakers, experience with Examples (21)-(22) directs their attention to the tract of land on which the school buildings stand and leads to a cross-linguistic difference in categorization of campus.

(21) I suppose somebody on the campus will know.

(22) There were no tall buildings on the campus. (BNC)

With diversity in cultural-specific experience, the boundaries of cognitive categories or the boundaries between typicality and atypicality vary across language communities. As was demonstrated in an array of studies on cross-linguistic difference in categorizing household objects (Malt, et al. 1999, 2003; Pavlenko & Malt 2011), the defining attributes related to a specific category were found to be different across the speakers from different native language backgrounds. For instance, in the study on the categorization of 60 common containers by native speakers of English, Spanish and Chinese, Malt, et al. (2003) administered the naming task and typicality rating tasks to the three groups of participants. The results indicated that the three groups varied in typicality judgments and identification of category membership with different attributes highlighted as the ones defining the category. Another good example was provided by Lipka (1987, cited in Ungerer & Schmid 2001: 51). In Figure 2.4, Furniture (b) is likely to be judged as a marginal member of the DESK category in the West or even in China. But in Japan or Korea where people conventionally sit at the desk with legs crossed, it will be considered as a prototypical desk (Ungerer & Schmid 2001: 51).

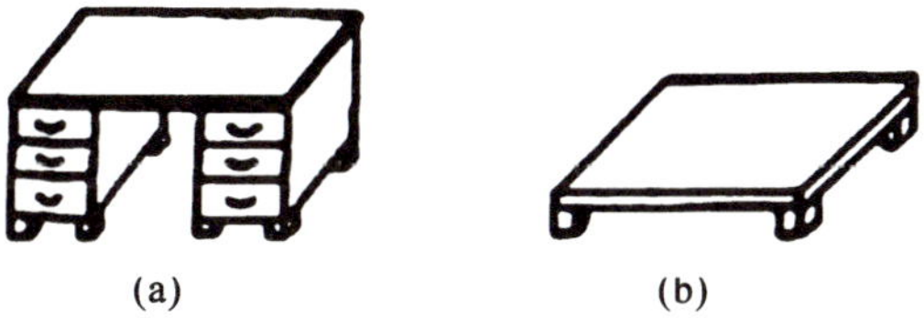

Figure 2.4 Illustration of European and Traditional Japanese Prototypes of the DESK Category (Lipka 1987: 292, cited in Ungerer & Schmid 2001: 51)

To sum up, categories are formed around prototype on the basis of family resemblance established by means of such basic cognitive operations as mental closure, conceptual projection across domains and topological characterization. By being culture-dependent, categories can be examined along two dimensions: Intralingual dimension and interlingual dimension. Within a speech community, the L1 acquired in childhood orients speakers to the aspects that are highlighted as the attributes defining the categories and leads to the development of L1-based category systems in which members are perceived to be representative to varying degrees depending on their distance with the prototype. Across speech communities, however, judgment of category membership and typicality is culture-specific to the extent that it is shared within a culture group but is always different across cultures. In accordance with the above assumptions on the nature of categorization, a definition of categories of reference objects is to be offered in the next part.

2.2.2 Prototype Approach to Categories of Reference Objects

In the domain of space, a reference object refers to the object "providing a reference point with respect to which the other object is situated" (Langacker 1987: 231). It was named as "Landmark" by Langacker (Langacker 1987: 231) which is functionally equivalent to Ground, a term borrowed from Gestalt psychology by Talmy (1983: 232). In the study, the term *reference object* is used to represent the actual instances of the objects that serve as reference points in a given spatial relation and the term *landmark* is employed to denote the abstraction of reference objects, or, in other words, the schematic image of reference objects.

In accordance with the assumptions of the formation of categories proposed by prototype theory, the categories of reference objects can be defined as the products of the categorization of the objects serving as reference points in a specific spatial relation by establishing resemblance between them and category prototypes through various mental operations. As shown in Figure 2.5, all the reference objects, namely envelope, saddle, moonlight, newspaper and queue, tend to be categorized as containers in English on the basis of family resemblance established by means of such mental operations as closing the material boundaries mentally or mapping conceptualization of one category onto another. This is well illustrated in Examples (23)-(27).

Figure 2. 5 Members of the CONTAINER Category

(23) He put the letter back in the envelope.

(24) His wife snapped, leaning forward in the saddle.

(25) Standing there in the moonlight, she looked magnificent.

(26) I saw a picture of you in the newspaper this morning.

(27) He was behind me in the queue. (BNC)

While the objects in different shapes and sizes cluster together in one category, they are, in terms of prototypicality, of different status as members of the CONTAINER category depending on their similarity to the prototype. The object envelope is most representative of the category by sharing maximum attributes with the prototype, whereas the object queue is a marginal member because of least resemblance to the prototype. In addition, the resemblance to the prototype is not only determined by the geometric attributes, but also by functional attributes (Coventry & Garrod 2004; Feist & Gentner 2012; Garrod, et al. 1999; Herskovits 1986; Vandeloise 1994). For instance, as shown in Figure 2. 6, though the bowl locates the pear inside geometrically, its function of containing gives place to that of covering when it is turned upside down. Subsequently, the bottom of the bowl is highlighted to the extent that the bowl is more accurately characterized as a covering surface corresponding with the landmark profiled by the preposition *under*.

Figure 2. 6 A Pear under the Bowl (Garrod, et al. 1999: 168)

As noted above, categories, being context-dependent, should also be examined cross-linguistically. Considering the cognitive apparatus universal to human beings, there are cross-linguistic similarities in categorizing objects. For example, both envelope and queue can also be categorized as containers in Chinese as illustrated by Examples (28)-(29) from Peking University-Center for Chinese Linguistics-Corpus (CCLC)①.

(28) 信封里有两张票。
xinfeng li you liang zhang piao.
envelope in have two pieces tickets
'There are two tickets in the envelope'.

(29) 我站在队伍里。
wo zhan zai duiwu li.
I stand at queue in
'I stand in the queue'.

However, for the other three objects in Figure 2.5, language-specific experience directs English and Chinese speakers to attend different aspects of the same objects and thereby causing cross-linguistic incongruity in categorization as shown by Examples (30)-(32) from CCLC.

(30) 曹操伏在马鞍上，直向舞阴逃去。
Cao Cao fu zai ma'an shang, zhi xiang Wuyin tao qu.
Cao Cao lean at saddle on straight direction Wuyin flee go
'Leaning forward in the saddle, Cao Cao fled to Wuyin'.

(31) 月光下亭亭地站着一个美人。
yueguang xia tingting de zhan-zhe yi ge mei ren.
moonlight under gracefully De_2 stand-DUR one CL beautiful person
'In the moonlight a beautiful lady is standing in a graceful manner'.

(32) 在报纸上见过几次他做的文章。
zai baozhi shang jian-guo ji ci ta zuo de wenzhang.
at newspaper on see-Exp several CL he do De_1 article
'His articles were seen in the newspaper several times'.

Taken together, categories of reference objects can be interpreted as follows: (1) Intralingually speaking, categories of reference objects mainly involve L1-based prototypicality of objects as reference points for the location

① Peking University-Center for Chinese Linguistics-Corpus is a monolingual corpus of Chinese constructed by Peking University, containing about 200 million Chinese characters. The corpus of modern Chinese, applied in the study, contains about 115 million Chinese characters.

of other objects, which is usually developed in the course of L1 acquisition; (2) Interlingually speaking, categories of reference objects involve the similarities and dissimilarities in judging the category membership and typicality of the reference objects across language communities.

The prototype approach to categories of reference objects acts as the basis for the following exploration of the effects of categorization of reference objects on the use of spatial prepositions.

2.3 Conceptual Transfer

Ever since the 1940s and the 1950s, when the groundbreaking work of Weinreich and Lado (Jarvis & Pavlenko 2008: 3) claimed for the importance of L1 transfer in L2 learning and investigated cases of transfer theoretically as a linguistic, psychological and sociological phenomenon (Jarvis & Pavlenko 2008: 5), the role and nature of transfer has been one of the hotly discussed issues in the field of L2 acquisition (Xu, et al. 2013). Just as Ellis (1999: 341) pointed out, "no theory of L2 acquisition is complete without an account of L1 transfer".

According to Jarvis and Pavlenko (2008: 5-6), studies of L1 transfer in L2 acquisition can be broadly divided into two research paradigms: Studying transfer as an explanans and studying transfer as an explanandum. In the first research paradigm, L1 transfer is regarded as a factor accounting for the process and result of L2 acquisition, and its fundamental objective is to identify to what extent L1 transfer affects second language acquisition. Three issues are of great concern to the researchers (Jarvis & Pavlenko 2008: 7): (1) Identifying cases of transfer taking place in L2 acquisition on the basis of comparative analysis; (2) Quantifying the transfer effects in comparison with other independent variables involved in L2 acquisition; (3) Specifying the scope of transfer in relation to the linguistic subsystems.

On the contrary, in the second research paradigm, L1 transfer is treated as a factor needing to be explained. Two research areas can be identified: Transferrability studies and conceptual transfer studies (Javis & Pavlenko 2008). In transferrability studies, researchers endeavor to explain how L1 transfer occurs in respect to linguistic, psychological and social constraints (Jarvis & Pavlenko 2008: 174). In the late 1970s, the failure of contrastive analysis in predicting the occurrence of L1 transfer (Ellis 1999) led researchers, most notably Selinker (1972), Ringbom (1978) and Kellerman (1979), to realize that cross-linguistic comparisons just indicate what might be transferred, but what actually will be transferred is likely to be influenced by various contextual factors and therefore, focus in transfer research was shifted from the description of L1 transfer to the exploration of in what conditions transfer occurs and does not occur (Larsen-Freeman & Long 2000: 96).

Conceptual transfer research is another important attempt to study transfer as an explanandum. It is intended to provide a cognitive explanation for the occurrence of transfer on the basis of "cross-linguistic similarities and dissimilarities in conceptual categories" (Jarvis & Pavlenko 2008: 112). As demonstrated in Levelt's speaking model (Levelt 1989, cited in de Bot 1992) capturing the process of language production, conceptualization of the world underlies language use by deciding what events are verbalized and how they are organized. Thus, research in this line is actually an attempt to reveal the mechanism of transfer at the interface between language and cognition (Jiang 2010: 166); to put it another way, it is an attempt to explain transfer in language use in terms of what learners think about reality.

As the attention is increasingly focused on the relationship between language and cognition, the last two decades have witnessed a fast development of conceptual transfer studies. In the following, the researcher initially presents the new theoretical developments in linguistics and psycholinguistics that promote the emergence of conceptual transfer studies, then, a comprehensive definition of conceptual transfer proposed by Jarvis (2011) is offered. Finally, a review of the previous studies on conceptual transfer is made.

2.3.1 New Theoretical Advances

A historic glance reveals that the ups and downs of transfer research are closely tied with the theoretical developments in linguistics, psychology and second language acquisition (Odlin 1989). The theoretical advances that propel the emergence of research on transfer as an explanandum mainly include Neo-Whorfianism and new developments in modeling bilingual conceptual representation.

Firstly, Neo-Whorfians' arguments on the relationship between language and cognition provide theoretical justification for conceptual transfer research linguistically (Jarvis & Pavlenko 2008: 15; Xu, et al. 2013: 104). Neo-Whorfianism, a term coined by Levinson (2003: 301), refers to a school of thought emerging in the late 1980s. Seeing the flaws in Chomsky's separation of language from cognition (Lakoff 1987: 58), Neo-Whorfianism made attempts to clarify and reevaluate Whorfian ideas on the relationship between language and thought by carrying out a spate of empirical studies to test the linguistic effects on users' categorization of the world (Chen 2011; Levinson 2003; Lucy 1997; Slobin 1996, 2000). While there was difference in research focus, they all claimed that a given language embodies a given interpretation of the reality and affects "patterns of thought about reality" (Lucy 1997: 294).

Much of the evidence for the first claim is from a series of studies on the cross-linguistic difference in spatial categorization between children with English and Korean as their first language respectively (Bowerman 1996a, 1996b, 2007; Bowerman & Choi 2003; Bowerman 2007; Choi 2006). As shown in Figures 2. 7 and 2. 8, a fundamental distinction is made in English between location at the interior of a specific reference object (e. g. , put book in case) and location at its boundary (e. g. , put cup on table), whereas in Korean the distinction is drawn between loose-fit (e. g. , put book in bag) and tight-fit relations (e. g. , put book in case) between the reference object and the located object (Bowerman 2007: 183-185).

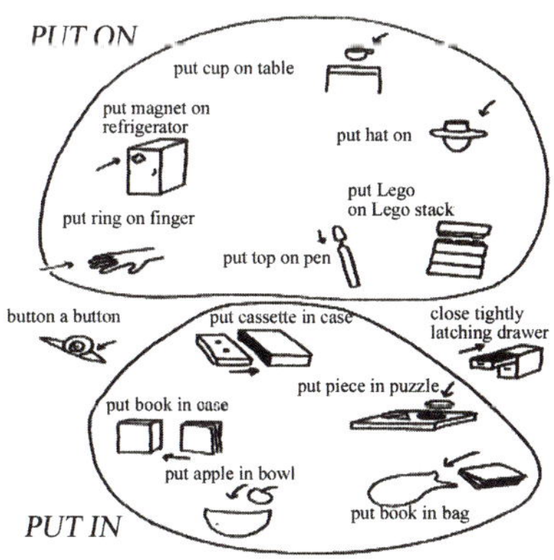

Figure 2. 7 Categorization of Spatial Events in English (Bowerman & Choi 2003: 313)

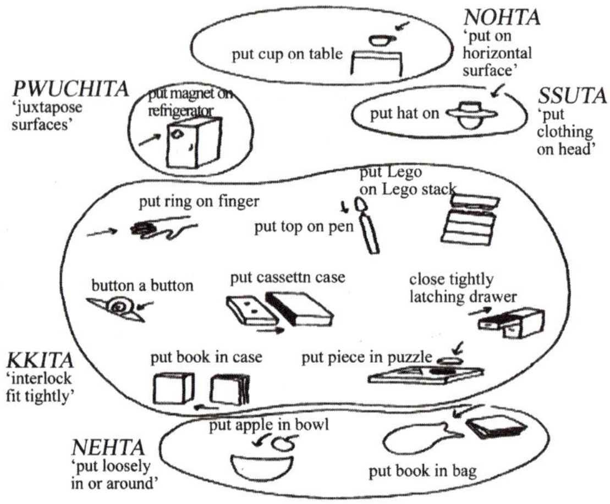

Figure 2.8 Categorization of Spatial Events in Korean (Bowerman & Choi 2003: 314)

The difference in conceptual distinction is attributed to the difference in the aspects that are highlighted in spatial categorization. For example, in English *book in case* and *book in bag* are in the same spatial category of CONTAINMENT with focus on whether the book is located inside the reference objects, but in Korean they are put in two different categories: TIGHT-FITTING CONTAINMENT and LOOSE-FITTING CONTAINMENT in accordance with whether the located object is inserted tightly or loosely into the reference objects. Researchers found that though there might exist universal spatial construal as argued by Jackendoff (1990), learning of L1 causes children of English and Korean to develop sensitivity to different aspects of spatial relations (Bowerman 2007: 193-194). Specifically speaking, English-speaking children pay more attention to the defining features relevant to containment or support, whereas Korean-speaking children maintain a high sensitivity to the distinction between tight-fit and loose-fit relations (Bowerman 2007: 194). Thus, the process of native language acquisition is also a process of acquisition of language-specific conceptualization of the world. As Slobin put it (1996: 91):

> The language or languages that we learn in childhood are not neutral coding systems of an objective reality. Rather each one is a subjective orientation to the world of human experience, and this orientation affects the ways in which we think while we are speaking.

It has been noted that conceptualization is fundamentally responsible for the content and form of a linguistic expression (Levelt 1989, cited in de Bot 1992), therefore the characteristic world-view residing in the language (Slobin 1996: 70) will in turn exert influences on users' production and comprehension of a verbal message. Such influence would stay in learning a second language (Odlin 2005: 5). Actually this has been mentioned by von Humboldt as early as 19th century:

> ...he (von Humboldt) sees second language acquisition as the only way an individual may escape from the conceptual world of the native language. Yet the escape is never, in the view of von Humboldt, completely successful: because "one always more or less carries over one's own world-, indeed one's own language-view, this success will not be felt to be pure and complete" (Odlin 2005: 7).

This suggests that before learners succeed in internalizing L2-based conceptual categories, learners' L2 behaviors are mostly rooted in L1-based conceptualization of the world. Therefore, it is of much necessity for researchers to examine learner language based on comparative studies in conceptualization which are contributory to revealing the deep-rooted cognitive mechanism of L1 transfer.

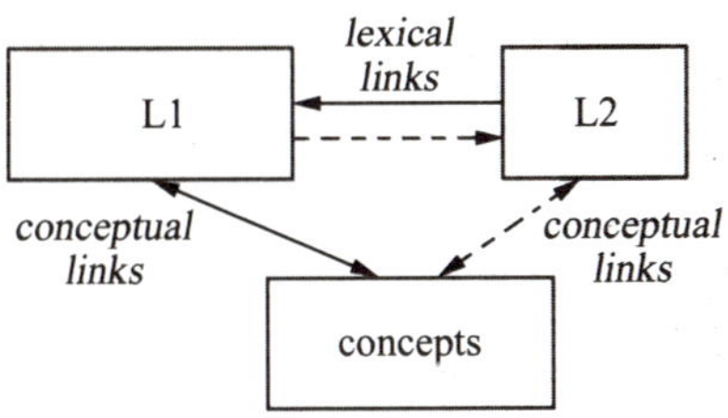

Figure 2.9 Revised Hierarchical Model of Lexical and Conceptual Representation in Bilingual Memory (Kroll & Stewart 1994: 158)

What drives the development of conceptual transfer research psychologically is the emergence of new models of bilingual conceptual representation in the 1990s (Jarvis & Pavlenko 2008: 17; Xu, Cai & Liu 2013: 104). Their arguments for the link between form and concept and the internal structure of bilingual conceptual representation provide psychological evidence for the conceptual source of transfer. Of the models conceived to capture the mappings of interlingual equivalents with concepts, Kroll and Stewart's (1994) Revised Hierarchical Model (RHM) (Figure 2.9) is the most notable. They integrated Word Association Model and Concept

Mediation Model① into a coherent one to capture the mental process of bilingual comprehension and production.

As shown in the model, interlingual equivalents are assumed to share one conceptual representation. Then, a question as to which form is more competitive in conceptual access arises. According to the model, at the beginning of L2 learning, the link between L1 words and concepts is stronger than that between L2 words and concepts. Only through "the mediation of the L1 equivalents", can the second language words gain conceptual access (Kroll & Stewart 1994: 166). This suggests that the conceptual representation of L2 words in this period is parasite on L1-mediated concepts (MacWhinney 2007: 81). Thus, the influence of L1-mediated concepts on learners' use of L2 words is unavoidable. But the model continued to point out that as L2 proficiency improves, the link between L2 words and concepts becomes stronger and the reliance on L1-mediated concepts will be gradually shaken off (Kroll & Stewart 1994: 167). This indicates that the improvement in L2 proficiency will result in a developmental variation of the effect of conceptual transfer.

Another important psychological evidence of conceptual transfer is from the models concerned with the internal structure of bilingual conceptual representation. Highly influential in this regard is Pavlenko's Modified Hierarchical Model (MHM) (Figure 2.10) (Pavlenko 2009). Drawing insight from the connectionist approach to bilingual representation (de Groot 1992; Dong & Gui 2002; Finkbeiner 2002; Li 2006), MHM assumes that bilingual conceptual representation is a compound comprising language-specific concepts and concepts universal to 2 languages (Pavlenko 2009: 146). When the conceptual link is established between L1-specific concepts and L2 words, interference from L1 will occur, but when the link is between the shared ones and L2 words, positive transfer will arise.

---

① According to Potter, et al. (1984: 23) and Kroll & Stewart (1994: 150), Word Association Model hypothesizes that new words in the second language are directly associated with the words in the first language and only through the mediation of the first language can the new words have access to the concepts, whereas, Concept Mediation Model assumes that new words in the second language are directly associated with the concepts without the mediation of the words in the first language.

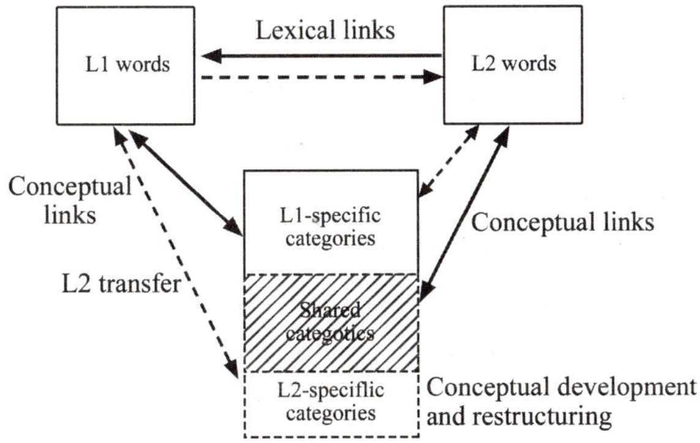

Figure 2. 10 Modified Hierarchical Model (Pavlenko 2009: 147)

Apparently, the two models illustrate how transfer occurs at the conceptual level and offer important psychological justifications for a conceptual approach to L1 transfer.

To recapitulate, with theoretical implications from the new advances in linguistics and psycholinguistics, the groundwork for tracing transfer back to the cognitive construal of the world is firmly established. Transfer research enters a new phase featured with the explorations of the conceptual impetus of the occurrence of transfer. For the purpose of elucidating the theoretical framework underlying conceptual transfer studies, Jarvis (2007, 2011) made attempts at defining conceptual transfer.

2.3.2 Definition of Conceptual Transfer

Transfer, with the unwelcome tag of "interference" being cast off, is currently defined as "the influence resulting from similarities and differences between the target language and any other language that has been previously (and perhaps imperfectly) acquired" (Odlin 1989: 27). In the present study, transfer mainly refers to the cross-linguistic influence generated by mother language, including positive transfer and negative transfer. Conceptual transfer, as a subpart of the system of language transfer, can be defined "at three different levels: as an observation, approach and hypothesis" according to Jarvis (2011: 1). To start with, as an observation, this term is used to refer to the observed cases of transfer that go beyond the structural and semantic properties of language and extend to the conceptualization of the world (Jarvis 2011: 2). Instances of such conceptual transfer were identified in the study of Chinese English learners' acquisition of English spatial prepositions by Li and Cai (2008). They found that learners sometimes misused the English preposition *from* as a replacement for *above* or *below*. The reason is that the spatial relations represented by *above* or *below* are sometimes categorized as distance relations in Chinese which are coded by the expression *cong... dao...* or *juli*, the translation equivalents of *from*. Secondly, as a new research approach to transfer, conceptual transfer research means explorations of transfer on the basis of recent empirical and theoretical developments in cognitive linguistics and cognitive psychology to find out the cognitive mechanism underlying the cross-linguistic influence in L2 learning (Jarvis 2011: 2). For example, Hohenstein, et al. (2006), based on Talmy's (1991) typological classification of lexicalization patterns of motion events, explored how the difference between Spanish (a verb-framed language) and English (a satellite-framed language) in conceptualization of motion events influenced the description of the motion events by Spanish-speaking English learners. Finally, as a hypothesis, Conceptual Transfer Hypothesis (CTH) states that certain instances of transfer in the use of L2 originate from the mental concepts and patterns of conceptualization that have been acquired in L1 learning (Jarvis 2011: 3). The empirical support can be found in the study by Graham and Belnap (1986) which showed that cross-linguistic differences in the internal make-up of the FURNITURE category might cause learners' linguistic categorization to diverge from that of natives. It can be seen that CTH is proposed on the basis of Linguistic Relativity Hypothesis (LRH) but simultaneously is different from LRH in that it extends the focus on the effect of language on cognition to the effect of cognition on language (Jarvis 2011: 3). To put it another way, it puts more emphasis on how the cognitive make-up formed in L1 learning affects L2 learning. The comprehensive definition of conceptual transfer at three different levels integrates various interpretations of conceptual transfer into a coherent unity and facilitates a systematic understanding of the objectives and methods of a conceptual approach to transfer research.

In accordance with Jarvis' three-level description of conceptual transfer, the study of conceptual transfer in the use of English spatial prepositions mainly includes: (1) Deriving testable hypotheses about the conceptual source of transfer from the developments of cognitive linguistics and cognitive psychology; (2) Collecting cases of transfer empirically to confirm or disconfirm the hypotheses.

Aside from the definition of conceptual transfer, Jarvis (2011) was also devoted to elucidating the abstract notion *concept*. Like transfer research in linguistic categories in which the linguistic categories are described as a set of features and comparative studies are conducted accordingly to identify the potential areas of transfer, conceptual transfer research also calls for a description of what a given conceptual category involves. Jarvis, in line with prototype theory (Rosch 1978), spelled out the components of concept as follows (Jarvis 2007: 52):

(1) a nucleus serving as the prototype of the conceptual category;
(2) typical images and schemas;
(3) peripheral images and schemas;
(4) knowledge components that are used to determine what can and cannot be categorized as a member;
(5) membership in a hierarchy of concepts.

The description of a conceptual category is significant in that it makes a conceptual category an observable and measurable phenomenon and provides theoretical guidance for comparative studies and for identification of sources of transfer at the conceptual level. Take the misuse of the preposition *through* in Example (5) in Section 1.1 as an instance. A comparison between the English expression and its corresponding Chinese translation in Example (33) reveals that the reference object denoted by *laugh* is construed as a member of the CONTAINER category, but the object denoted by its Chinese equivalent *xiao sheng* is construed as a container serving as a path (Talmy 2000). According to Jarvis, there is difference in "membership in a hierarchy of concepts" between *laugh* and *xiao sheng*. To be precise, the two concepts represented by *laugh* and *xiao sheng* are not at the same level of categorization with the category of CONTAINER AS A PATH being subordinate to the CONTAINER category. The use of the spatial preposition *through* in Example (5) indicates that learners under the influence of L1 construed the perception event as a fictive motion event (Talmy 2000: 115-116) and *laugh* as a container functioning as a path. Thus, the reason for the misuse of *through* is identified.

(33) In her childish laugh, he recognized the tones of little Pearl.
从她童稚的笑声中他辨出了小珠儿的腔调。(GCEPC)①

In the study, the cross-linguistic comparison in categorization of reference objects between English and Chinese and the explanation of conceptual mechanism of L1 transfer in the use of English spatial prepositions by L2 learners are made in the light of Jarvis' description of what a conceptual category includes.

In the following, a review of previous empirical studies of conceptual transfer is made in an attempt to reveal the achievements that have been made and to identify the gaps in current research.

2.3.3 Empirical Studies of Conceptual Transfer

Before the 1990s, there were few pioneering empirical studies on the transfer from the native language-mediated concepts (Clarke, et al. 1981; Ijaz 1986). For example, Clarke, et al. (1981) conducted a study on conceptual transfer in the domain of gender with Arabic learners of English as a second language. Typological studies revealed that Arabic is a language having "maximum gender loading in which gender is marked obligatorily for all nouns and their modifiers" (Clarke, et al. 1981: 159), but in English, gender is only assigned to the nouns denoting animated beings (Jarvis & Pavlenko 2008: 132). In a semantic differential test composed of a masculine-feminine scale and three sets of stimulus words, learners were observed to construe the sexual connotation of English words mostly based on how their Arabic equivalents are marked linguistically in terms of gender. This indicates that L1-based gender assignment locks learners into a particular pattern of conceptualization of gender, which in turn affects their acquisition of gender assignment in English. Similar findings were reported by Ijaz's (1986) study on the conceptual transfer

① General Chinese-English Parallel Corpus (GCEPC) is a bidirectional parallel corpus constructed by Professor Wang and his colleagues in 2004, containing about 20 million English words and Chinese characters. The corpus applied in the study contains about 3.5 million English words.

in acquisition of English prepositions. While the two studies were found to be problematic in focusing on the semantic relationship between words rather than the relationship between words and their referents, they kicked off more in-depth studies of conceptual transfer.

Since the 1990s, more empirical conceptual transfer studies have been undertaken and exhibited the following three characteristics: (1) The scope of studies is greatly expanded; (2) Negative conceptual transfer receives much focus; (3) Nonverbal tasks and visual prompts are widely used to increase the validity of research.

As Jarvis and Pavlenko (2008: 122) claimed, conceptual transfer research in the last two decades has covered eight basic conceptual domains: Objects (Cook, et al. 2006; Malt & Sloman 2003; Pavlenko & Malt 2011), emotions (Pavlenko 2002; Pavlenko & Driagina 2007), personhood (Churchill & DuFon 2006), gender (Dewaele & Véronique 2001; Holmes & Dejean de la Batie 1999), number (Yang 2014; Yoon 1993), time (Boroditsky 2001; Slobin 1996), space (Becker & Carroll 1997; Li & Cai 2008; Xu, Liu & Cai 2014; Zhang & Liu 2013) and motion (Daller, et al. 2011; Hohenstein, et al. 2006; Xu 2013). In these studies, the potential areas of transfer were usually identified in the first place on the basis of typological or comparative studies of the universals or diversities across languages in representing a given concept. Then, empirical studies were conducted to test the predicated transfer effects in the use of L2 structures. For instance, in Yang's (2014) study of L1 transfer in the comprehension and production of English plurals by Chinese learners of English as a second language, a comparative analysis between English and articleless languages reveals that in the articleless languages like Chinese, bare plurals can be used to represent both generic reference and definite reference, but in English, bare plurals are confined to generic reference and definite reference is encoded by definite plurals. Against this background, the hypotheses about how L1 transfer happens were put forward as follows: (1) Chinese learners have little difficulty in comprehending generic reference of English bare plurals and simultaneously overaccept their definite reference; (2) They have much difficulty in comprehending and producing English definite plurals headed by the definite article *the*. The statistical analysis of the learner data elicited by the truth value judgment task and the error correction task confirmed both positive transfer and negative transfer of L1 as predicted.

While positive transfer received much attention, research in the eight conceptual domains, propelled by Neo-Whorfianism findings of cross-linguistic diversities in conceptualization, was primarily concerned with negative transfer (Jarvis & Pavlenko 2008: 112). In accordance with whether the concept is lexicalized or grammaticized (Jarvis & Pavlenko 2008: 115), two types of negative transfer can be identified: (1) Transfer in lexical choice; (2) Transfer in syntactic choice. In the explorations of conceptual mechanism of transfer in lexical choice, much attention was directed at semantic confusion. Researchers attempted to explain the semantic transfer on the basis of cross-linguistic differences in conceptual distinctions. For example, in the study of Chinese learners' use of English spatial prepositions, Li and Cai (2008) found that learners sometimes used the preposition *on* inappropriately as a replacement for *in* or *at*. Comparative studies revealed that the object concepts profiled by the three prepositions are subsumed under one conceptual category SURFACE in Chinese. Without internalization of the finer distinctions made in English, the object concept SURFACE was projected onto the preposition *on* and as a result, the semantic range of *on* was erroneously extended. The study casts new light on the conceptual mechanism of semantic confusion in the use of L2 words by tracing semantic transfer to the difference in conceptualization of the reference object. However, such attempts have been rare until now.

The final feature is concerned with methodology of conceptual transfer studies. To enhance the validity of data on the effects of the language-specific concepts on learners' use of L2, the empirical studies of conceptual transfer mainly involved learners in the following three types of tasks: Categorization, naming and picture-elicited verbalization (Jarvis 2007: 58-59; Pavlenko 2009: 130-131). These tasks are advantageous in "holding the semantic referent constant" (Jarvis & Pavlenko 2008: 312) and eliciting convincing evidence for "conceptual-related differences without being confounded by patterns of language use" (Jarvis 2007: 59). Categorization and naming were usually preferred in research on domains involving categorization of concrete objects, whereas in research on the domains of emotion, space or time that cannot be categorized like concrete objects, picture-elicited verbal tasks were more popularly used, in which learners were asked to retell a story or to output a language feature under investigation while looking at a series of pictures or a video segment (Pavlenko 2009: 131). In the study of the effect of L1-specific conceptualization of motion events on the use of L2 verbs, Hohenstein, et al. (2006) elicited learners' production of verbs by asking the Spanish-speaking learners of English from two proficiency groups to watch 12 video clips. The clips involved six different paths of motion (e. g. , entering, exiting, crossing, going uphill, going downhill and going into a pool), each of which included two different manners of motion. For example,

(34) girl *twirling* out of the building

(35) girl *walking* out of the building

After watching the video, the participants were required to say as much as they could in English under the guidance of the two general questions: (1) What is he/she doing? (2) What is happening? By comparing the verbs and manner modifiers used in narration between bilingual learners and Spanish and English monolinguals, the researchers found that learners, like Spanish monolinguals, showed less preference for verbs of manner and manner modifiers than English monolinguals. This confirmed the influence of Spanish-specific insensitivity to manner in conceptualization of motion events (Slobin 1996) on learners' choice of English verbs. And simultaneously, as reported in other transfer studies, the more experienced learners were observed to suffer less from conceptual transfer with production of more verbs of manner. This demonstrates that the increasing exposure to L2 input results in the development of learners' sensitivity to manner of motion and provides empirical evidence for the conceptual change taking place in the process of L2 acquisition.

To sum up, transfer research in the last two decades has made great strides in developing a concept-oriented approach to the investigation of transfer as an explanandum (Jarvis & Pavlenko 2008). It pushes the explanation of L1 transfer to the language-specific construal of reality and helps in finding out the cognitive basis of non-native use of L2 forms by learners. This apparently has important implications for foreign language teaching. However, some questions still need to be discussed further.

Firstly, as Saussure (1983: 121, cited in Chandler 2004: 22) has argued, the meaning of a linguistic sign is not determined by its "inherent features" but by its systematic relations with other things that surround it. In other words, the meaningful output of a word is highly correlated with the words that are in a syntactic relation with it. Thus, the probe into the mechanism of semantic transfer should not be confined to the conceptual representation of the word in isolation but extends to the conceptualizations of the words collocating with it, especially in the studies of transfer in the acquisition of relational predicates. As reported in the study by Li and Cai (2008), the misuse of the preposition *on* was triggered by the difference in conceptual representation between English nouns and their Chinese equivalents. However, as mentioned above, few attempts have been made in this aspect.

Secondly, while Pavlenko (2009) proposed a finer look at the language distance, most studies still tended to classify language distance into two types: Similarity and difference in their comparative studies. Actually conceptual contrast between the translation equivalents is far more complicated. Between equivalence and non-equivalence, there are different types of partial equivalence which have different effects on the occurrence of L1 transfer. Therefore, a more complete contrastive analysis is needed to draw a continuum of cross-linguistic equivalence in conceptualization, on the basis of which a more comprehensive explanation of the mechanism of L1 transfer can be made.

Thirdly, most of conceptual transfer studies were conducted in natural L2 learning settings, which are quite different from instructional settings in terms of the amount and quality of L2 input. Especially in discussing the effect of L2 proficiency on conceptual transfer, the advanced learners selected usually had resided in the target nation several years. Therefore, their findings cannot well explain the occurrence of L1 transfer observed in the instructional context where L1 is a dominant language.

2.4 Studies of L2 Acquisition of English Spatial Prepositions

In English, spatial prepositions usually refer to a class of words denoting the locative relationship between two objects. Since spatial perception is one of the most fundamental human experiences, English spatial prepositions play an indispensable role in spatial contextualization of an utterance. However, the polysemous nature of prepositions and the partial overlapping between English prepositions and their interlingual equivalents cause English prepositions to be notoriously difficult to learn for L2 learners (Ma 2007). As a consequence, acquisition of English prepositions by L2 learners draws much attention from L2 acquisition researchers. A historical glance at the previous studies reveals that there are fundamentally two approaches to this issue: Descriptive approach and cognitive approach. The descriptive approach is aimed at showing learners' preference for English prepositions, whereas the cognitive one seeks to find out the underlying constraints that govern learners' preference within the framework of cognitive linguistics. The following section is intended to review the two approaches to the empirical studies of acquisition of English spatial prepositions.

2.4.1 Descriptive Studies of L2 Acquisition of English Spatial Prepositions

As regards the descriptive studies of the acquisition of English spatial prepositions by L2 learners (Gui 2005; Khampang 1974; Mougeon, et al. 1979; Oller, et al. 1971; Pavesi 1987; Schumann 1986), three issues with respect to the use of prepositions have captured the attention of researchers: (1) Learners' preferential selections of certain prepositions over others; (2) Developmental sequence in L2 acquisition of prepositions; (3) Variability in using prepositions.

The first issue constitutes the starting point for the research on acquisition of English spatial prepositions. In the studies of learners' preferential selections of prepositions, learners' production of prepositions was elicited by tests or verbal tasks or was taken from learner corpus. Then, the patterns in learners' use of prepositions were identified in terms of errors, overuse or avoidance in comparison with English native speakers. A good example in this regard is Gui's corpus-based description of Chinese learners' use of English prepositions (Gui 2005). Chinese Learner English Corpus (CLEC) was selected as the study corpus and two English corpora of native speakers, FLOB and FROWN, were selected as the reference corpora. A comparison was made in the frequency of the prepositions and the type/token ratio. The patterns in the use of prepositions by Chinese learners were reported as follows: (1) Learners tended to overuse the prepositions that were frequently used by English native speakers, like *in* and tended to underuse the prepositions that were of low frequency, like *across*; (2) Learners' use of prepositions lacked variety with low type/token ratio. Gui's research is one of the few attempts to provide a comprehensive picture of learners' preferential choices of English prepositions without focusing on errors.

However, in the empirical studies of the developmental sequence and variation in L2 acquisition of prepositions, Error Analysis was still a major research paradigm. Based on the analysis of errors, like the quantification of errors and examination of the sources of errors, researchers endeavored to investigate whether preposition acquisition proceeds in a fixed order and shows systematic variability under various contextual constraints.

Much of the earlier work emerging around the 1970s (Khampang 1974; Mougeon, et al. 1979; Oller, et al. 1971) focused on the order of L2 acquisition of English prepositions. This is mainly attributed to the popularity of the Universal Grammar approach to L2 acquisition in that period (Ellis 1999). Central to these studies was usually the sought for the empirical evidence of the developmental sequence to the neglect of the importance of L1 transfer in L2 acquisition of prepositions. To this end, errors were collected and quantified as evidence of the order of acquisition, and three types of comparisons were commonly made: (1) A comparison of the syntactic and semantic features of prepositions between L1 and L2; (2) A comparison of errors between L1 learners and L2 learners; (3) A comparison of errors among L2 learners from different native language backgrounds.

In a pioneering study on Thai-speaking learners' acquisition of English prepositions, Khampang (1974) collected errors through a diagnostic test consisting of three parts: Multiple choice, error correction and cloze test. To investigate whether the errors were specific to Thai learners, he also administered the test to English learners from Japan, Spain and other countries. On the basis of cross-linguistic comparisons between English and Thai and statistical comparisons of frequency of learner errors in using English prepositions across the groups from different native language background, the researcher found that although there was some evidence of L1 transfer, the frequency of errors across the groups was not significantly different. This suggests that native language background does not exert significant effect on the learners' use of English prepositions and the universal developmental sequence is empirically supported.

Similar findings were reported by Mougeon, et al. (1979) in their study of the spoken production of English prepositions by bilingual Ontarian learners. Different from Khampang (1974), Mougeon, et al. made a comparison of errors between monolingual and bilingual learners, in which the order of preposition acquisition was observed to be essentially the same between the two groups of learners. As to more errors found in the use of the two prepositions *to* and *into* by bilingual children, Mougeon, et al. (1979: 25) attributed them to the interference of French on the basis of the identification of the semantic differences between the French preposition *a* and the misused English prepositions *in* and *at*. However, they simultaneously pointed out that L1 just retarded the acquisition of the 2 prepositions and did not affect the order of acquisition.

It can be seen that in the earlier studies on preposition acquisition, the importance of the universal developmental sequence was emphasized to the extent that the role of L1 transfer in acquisition of prepositions was minimized (Ellis 1999: 309).

Variation in the use of L2 English prepositions is another issue that has received much attention since the 1980s (Pavesi 1987; Schumann1986). Variation research primarily deals with the description of patterns of variation in relation to the linguistic, psychological and social constraints. Of the constraints in focus, L1 transfer was always put at the forefront. A good example was provided by Schumann (1986), who investigated the effects of cross-linguistic similarities and differences in semantics and syntax on the use of locative and directional expressions by English learners from Spain, Japan and China. Three important findings concerning L1 transfer were reported: (1) The merge of the two linguistic categories *in* and *on* into one category *en* in Spanish caused the Spanish-speaking learners to overuse *in* while describing locative relations; (2) The absence of prepositions in description of motion events in Chinese led to the omission of the preposition *to* in Chinese learners' directional expressions; (3) Although there is cross-linguistic syntactic similarity in describing locative relations between English and the first languages, Chinese and Japanese, the learners from the two native language backgrounds still tended to omit the locative prepositions. Regarding the last finding, Schumann (1986: 285) did not attribute it to the inhibition of L1 positive transfer but to the strategy of simplification that was used in both L1 and L2 learning. The conclusion was hasty in that the omission of prepositions was observed to be context dependent because prepositions were more likely to be omitted when learners put the locative expressions at the head of the sentence and took the reference object as the topic. Thus, it might be reasonable to assume that the syntactic context inhibits the occurrence of positive transfer and leads to the omission of prepositions.

The descriptive studies of L2 acquisition of English prepositions sketch a picture of the preferential selections of English prepositions by L2 learners from different L1 backgrounds and serve as a prelude to the cognitive studies of acquisition of English prepositions. The patterns identified in the descriptive studies push researchers to generate hypotheses on the cognitive factors affecting learners' use of prepositions and to conduct empirical studies to test their hypotheses in hopes of uncovering the deep-seated mechanism underlying the production of prepositions. Actually, as shown in the foregoing discussion, much effort has been made to identify the factors accounting for the errors in learners' use of prepositions, like L1 transfer or simplification (Schumann 1986: 293).

Despite the great achievements, the descriptive studies are also found problematic in their minimalist approach to L1 transfer (Ellis 1999: 309) in acquisition of English spatial prepositions. The minimalist position on L1 transfer found expression in two ways: L1 was believed to exert little influence on the order of acquisition of English spatial prepositions, though sometimes it was observed to "delay or speed up passage through the developmental sequence" (Larsen-Freeman & Long 2000: 96; Mougeon, et al. 1979); (2) L1 transfer was viewed as merely one of learning strategies to overcome the difficulties caused by the L2 knowledge gap (Ellis 1999: 314). When transfer did not happen as predicated by contrastive analysis, another strategy was usually claimed to work and little account was taken of the constraints governing L1 transfer (Schumann 1986).

Another problem with the descriptive studies is that L2 acquisition of semantic features of English spatial prepositions was not given due attention. For one thing, in analyzing learner errors, no distinction was made between syntactic errors and semantic errors. Since the studies on the developmental patterns of learner language usually put an overemphasis on morphology and syntax, the conclusion that learning of prepositions proceeds in a universal order with little interference from L1 might not hold true for the development of semantic representations of English prepositions. For another thing, though some researchers like Mougeon, et al. (1979) or Schumann (1986) addressed the issue of the acquisition of semantics, there was a lack of detailed semantic analysis, including both the intralingual comparisons of semantic representations across the prepositions and the interlingual comparisons between English prepositions and their translation equivalents. Without an in-depth analysis, instances of transfer couldn't be fully recognized, and quantification of the transfer effects in comparison with other independent variables involved in L2 acquisition was not reliable. More importantly, researchers couldn't possibly dig out the deep-seated cognitive factors causing learners to produce the spatial expressions that are syntactically good but semantically odd.

Since the 1980s, with a growing concern over the relationship between language and cognition, there emerges a cognitive approach to L2 acquisition of semantic systems of English spatial prepositions which seeks to uncover the cognitive mechanism underlying the preferential use of English spatial prepositions by learners of English as a second language.

2.4.2 Cognitive Studies of L2 Acquisition of English Spatial Prepositions

The studies of L2 acquisition of English spatial prepositions are cognitive in that they are intended to provide an account for the use of English spatial prepositions by L2 learners on the basis of analyzing the conceptual nature of semantics of prepositions by cognitive linguistics.

Different from the earlier work, a noteworthy feature of the cognitive studies of preposition acquisition is that, stimulated by the resurgence of interest in transfer research since the 1980s (Larsen-Freeman &Long 2000: 97) and by the revelation of the cross-linguistic diversities in spatial conceptualization in Neo-Whorfianism studies (Jarvis & Pavlenko 2008: 142), more emphasis was put on L1 transfer in explaining the semantic confusion in the use of English spatial prepositions. An important subset of this strand of research is the exploration of the cognitive underpinnings of transfer from the perspective of spatial categorization, which can be further divided into two research paradigms in accordance with the level at which comparative studies in spatial categorization were conducted.

In the first paradigm (Correa-Beningfield 1985; Ijaz 1986; Ma 2007; Young-Davy 2000), concepts tend to be equated with semantics of spatial prepositions and L1 transfer was attributed to the similarities and differences in semantic structures between English spatial prepositions and their translation equivalents. But for the second research paradigm, L1 transfer was traced back to the conceptual representation of spatial prepositions (Becker & Carroll 1997; Jarvis & Odlin 2000; Li & Cai 2008; Xu, et al. 2014; Zhang & Liu 2013). Attempts were made to visualize the spatial concepts and cross-linguistic contrast in terms of image schema or perceptual experience (Jarvis & Pavlenko 2008).

A review of literature reveals that in the first research paradigm, prototypicality of semantic members within a spatial category was always investigated as an important factor in governing the occurrence of L1 transfer. The interest in the effect of prototypicality is largely attributed to the emergence of the prototype approach to the polysemous nature of prepositions (Lakoff 1987; Langacker 1987; Taylor 2002). While there were a variety of proposals on the process of semantic extension, they all shared the basic tenet of prototype-based categorization: The members of a semantic category have different degrees of typicality and are linked with each other by family resemblance (Li 2008: 99). The typical semantic members share the maximum attributes with prototype and have been empirically tested to be the first ones acquired by children (Gentner & Bowerman 2009; Kelly 2002; Xu 2010). This pushed many researchers to study whether the effect of prototypicality also occurs in L2 acquisition of prepositions. Particularly important in this regard are the two studies by Correa-Beningfield (1985) and Ma (2007).

Correa-Beningfield (1985) might be one of the pioneers to make a brave attempt at the effect of prototypicality on acquisition of English spatial prepositions by L2 learners. One striking feature of his study is that he showed concern for the interaction between prototypicality and cross-linguistic similarities by raising the prototypicality transfer hypothesis: "The English preposition that corresponds most closely in its prototype concept to the prototype concept of a given Spanish preposition would tend to be preferred by Spanish speakers learning English to other prepositions" (Correa-Beningfield 1985: 60). To test the hypothesis, four English spatial prepositions were selected: *in*, *on*, *at* and *over*. The four semantic categories are coalesced into two categories *en* and *sobre* respectively in Spanish, as diagrammed in Figure 2. 11:

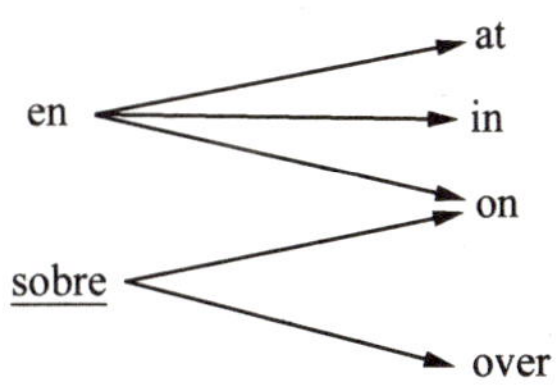

Figure 2. 11 Overlap between Spanish Prepositions and English Prepositions (Correa-Beningfield 1985: 8)

Two prototype tests were administered to English native students and Spanish learners of English to elicit their ranking for prototypicality of the various uses of the prepositions under study, and after that, two cloze tests were performed to collect learners' use of English spatial prepositions. One more point worth mentioning was that considering the presence of Spanish expressions in the translation cloze test would promote L1 transfer, the study attached pictures to the cloze test to offset the potential interference of the Spanish expressions.

The results indicated that the hypothesized interaction between prototypicality and L1 transfer was largely supported with the occurrence of both strong positive transfer and negative transfer. Specifically speaking, the correspondence in prototype between *in* and *en* and *on* and *sobre* facilitated learners' correct choice of *in* or *on*, but simultaneously inhibited the choice of other equivalents that are more appropriate in a given context. This indicates that there is an erroneous extension of the semantic categories of the prepositions *in* and *on* caused by their overlapping with L1 equivalents in prototypical members. The study by Correa-Beningfield is significant in that:

(1) It firstly empirically established the prototype concept for the prepositions and verified the prototype-based categorization of semantic members within a category; (2) The confirmation of prototype transfer hypothesis reveals prototypicality is an important cognitive mechanism of L1 transfer observed in the use of English spatial prepositions and simultaneously provides evidence of the involvement of both L1 and L2 spatial semantic systems in the acquisition of English spatial prepositions.

However, the study is still found problematic in the following two aspects. Firstly, it just focused on the effect of prototypical senses and did not take non-prototypical senses into consideration. The non-prototypical senses, especially peripheral ones, are usually where the semantic categories of prepositions overlap each other and are also where L1 and L2 diverge from each other in semantic categorization (Ijaz 1986; Ma 2007), thus, they will pose more challenges to L2 learners and their effects on acquisition of English prepositions will be much more complicated than the prototypical ones. In addition, the importance of prototype effects on learner's use of English prepositions cannot be highlighted unless a comparison of the effects between the prototypical members and the non-prototypical members is made (Ma 2005: 43). Therefore, a complete account of the prototype effects should take all the members of different degrees of prototypicality into consideration.

Secondly, the study did not probe into the effect of L2 proficiency. With L2 acquisition being a developmental process (Ellis 1999: 73), L2 proficiency must be an important factor accounting for the variation in learner language. Bilingual research also reveals that the link between language form and concept is highly correlated with L2 proficiency (Kroll & Stewart 1994). As hypothesized in RHM (Kroll & Stewart 1994), L2 words are connected with concepts only through the mediation of their L1 equivalents at earlier stages of L2 learning, whereas with the development of L2 proficiency, L2 words will have direct access to the concepts without the mediation of their L1 equivalents. This suggests that L2 proficiency will has an effect on L1 transfer in learners' semantic representations of English prepositions, which will in turn exert influence on prototype effects. This necessitates the involvement of L2 proficiency in transfer studies.

These problems were well solved in Ma's (2007) study which focused on the acquisition of the three spatial prepositions, *in*, *on* and *over*. Firstly, based on the previous studies, the researcher classified the semantic members within each semantic category into three levels: prototypical, intermediate and peripheral, and examined how prototypicality of senses interacted with L1 transfer in affecting Chinese learners' acquisition of English spatial prepositions. Secondly, a comparison of learners' performance across different proficiency groups was made to discover whether the increase in L2 proficiency would promote the development of L2 spatial concepts. Two important findings were reported: (1) The core semantic members are usually where cross-linguistic convergence in categorization lies and therefore, pose little difficulty for learners, whereas the peripheral members are usually where L1 and L2 diverge in categorization and, in this case, learners tend to carry the L1-based semantic boundaries over to L2; (2) The increase in L2 proficiency does not always promote the development in L2 spatial concepts and result in a reduction of negative transfer effects, because the significant difference in L2 performance was not observed between the intermediate learners and the advanced learners.

Ma's study is a more in-depth exploration of the cognitive factors accounting for the misuse of English spatial prepositions by L2 learners and provides important insight into the mechanism of semantic transfer. In addition, the exploration of the effect of L2 proficiency shed some light on the relationship between L2 learning and the development of L2-based concepts in classroom-based L2 learning context.

But the study also suffered from some weaknesses. Firstly, similar to most of the studies in this field, the research focus was set on the decontextualized semantic representations of prepositions and little regard was given to the fact that prepositions function as relational predicates (Langacker 1987: 215) whose semantic properties are closely related to the words that keep company with them. As illustrated in Examples (36)-(38), the containers denoted by the three nouns, *man*, *queue* and *sun* are different in physical and functional attributes and as a result, the semantic representations for the three instances of *in* involve different feature bundles (Ma 2005):

(36) a man in the room: [containment]+[full enclosure]+[full occluding]

(37) a man in the queue: [part-whole]+[partial enclosure]+[non occluding]

(38) a man in the sun: [full enclosure]+[non occluding]

As mentioned in Introduction, the conceptualization of the objects connected by the prepositions assigns semantic values to prepositions (Cuyckens 1993; Hottenroth 1993; Langacker 1987). This implies that learners' construal of the nouns collocating with the prepositions is an important cognitive basis of the appropriate selection of prepositions. It then follows that the textual context has an important role to play in permitting or inhibiting L1 transfer (Jarvis & Pavlenko 2008: 189). However, such constraints have not yet received much attention except for a few attempts at confirming the influence of L1 collocational patterns in English preposition learning (Koosha & Jafarpour 2006).

Secondly, though the study was claimed to unveil how L1-based spatial categorization influences learners' use of English spatial prepositions, the investigation was still limited to the semantic system of language rather than users' construal of the spatial layout. In the study, the spatial concepts represented by prepositions were described as a bundle of objective semantic features. Jarvis and Pavlenko (2008: 118) ever stated that semantic representation is the mapping of conceptual representation onto the word. To put it another way, the semantic representation is the product of users' spatial categorization rather than spatial categorization itself, or in Zelinsky-Wibbelt's (1993: 15) words, "the parameters which are part of the semantic representation of the preposition are assigned values by being mapped onto the conceptual representation of the reference object". Take the core sense of *in* as an example (Ma 2007: 175).

[containment]+ [full enclosure] +[full occluding]

The combination of the three features indicates that the speaker categorizes the reference object as a container in which a located object is fully enclosed and occluded. But how the object is perceived as such a container, or, in other words, how a given reference object in all its bulk and physicality is boiled down to a mental image of container, is still unknown. Therefore, equating the spatial categorization with the semantic representation and confining the cross-linguistic difference in spatial categorization to the difference in semantic structures evidently cannot reveal the deep-rooted cognitive mechanism underlying the use of spatial prepositions. Since the 1990s, increasing attention has been paid to L1 transfer at the conceptual level.

Becker and Carroll (1997) might be the first to make an attempt at a conceptual approach to L2 learners' acquisition of English spatial prepositions. This can be clearly seen in their framework of analysis: "The spatial concepts pertaining to the construal of the geometrical and functional features of objects connected by the prepositions are one of the cognitive prerequisites for processing the spatial expressions" (Becker & Carroll 1997: 13).

Before an empirical research was conducted, a theoretical justification for the research was made in the following two aspects: (1) An illustration of the conceptual underpinning of spatial prepositions; (2) A comparison of the cross-linguistic differences in conceptualization of space. With a division between object-based and axis-based spatial structuring, a detailed analysis of spatial concepts underlying the senses of the spatial prepositions was made (Becker & Carroll 1997: 38). For example, the location of Object A at the interior subspace of the reference object constitutes the conceptual basis of the basic sense of *in*, whereas *in front of* means that Object A is located at the frontal subspace of the reference object which is defined by the front axis with respect to the orientation of the observer (Becker & Carroll 1997: 27-28).

As to the differences in spatial conceptualization between Italian and English, the researchers argued that finer distinctions of subspaces are made in English and there tends to be an alternation between object-based and axis-based conceptualization of space, but Italian relies more on the axes without a mediating object part and does not care whether the subspaces are interior or exterior to the reference object or along the vertical or sagittal axis (Becker & Carroll 1997: 38). Specifically speaking, when the location of the object is interior to the reference object, or the exterior subspace is structured via the sagittal axis, English will give more prominence to the object-based conceptualization of space. This implies the production of English spatial coding system is based to a large degree on users' construal of the inherent features of objects and the subspaces defined by objects (Becker & Carroll 1997: 38). As such, there will be an alternation in English between *on* and *above* in accordance with whether the located object is at a boundary or an exterior subspace of the reference object. However, the Italian equivalent *su* can be applied to either of the above two spatial relations (Becker & Carroll 1997: 38). Secondly, English will use the nouns denoting the inherent parts of the reference object to structure subspaces along the vertical axis, like *on the top*, in contrast, Italian will opt for the axis-based expression, like *nel di sopra* (*in the above*) (Becker & Carroll 1997: 39).

Based on the above findings, a two-year longitudinal study was conducted on two Italian immigrants in England in hopes of identifying the factors, including the L1-related factors that constrain L2 development in a natural learning environment. Two narrative tasks, stage direction and picture description, were specifically designed for eliciting the participants' spatial reference and description. With an in-depth analysis of the types and tokens of spatial expressions used by learners during the two years, the researchers found that cross-linguistic divergence in conceptualization of space figured much in both participants' acquisition of English spatial expressions. For instance, Vito was confused with the inconsistency in the pattern of spatial structuring in English and failed to use the object-based spatial expressions properly, as demonstrated in Example (39) (Becker & Carroll 1997: 69):

(39) in reporting that money is hidden under the table

Vito: not in top (of the table)

As mentioned above, axis-based expressions in English apply to an exterior space along the vertical axis. In Example (39), the money was located at a lower-exterior subspace delimited by the table and the axis-based expression *under* was preferred.

As to Santo, he insistently used axis-based spatial expressions in his earlier years in England because of the interference of L1. For example (Becker & Carroll 1997: 66, 71),

(40) in referring to a book put down on the table

Santo: the book in the up this +/yeah upstairs the table

(41) in explaining the direction the mugger took

Santo: the park/twenty five meter behind the park in the left...

But in the last phase of data collection, object-based forms were found to be used by Santo in replacement of the axis-based ones. For example (Becker & Carroll 1997: 73),

(42) in directing his partner to draw a chimney on the roof

Santo: okay now I forget one point over this house have the camino (chimney)

This indicates that in the course of socialization into English community, conceptual transfer from Italian is gradually weakened with the increase in L2 learning experience.

Of the studies on L2 learners' acquisition of English spatial prepositions, Becker and Carroll's study is particularly important in that it made a brave attempt at the analysis of the conceptual nature of spatial semantics and at the cross-linguistic comparison of spatial conceptualization in terms of visual images rather than a bundle of semantic features. More importantly, the study reveals that object concept in English is an important mechanism underlying the use of English spatial prepositions and provides a significant insight for the conceptual research approach to L1 transfer in L2 learners' acquisition of English spatial expressions. In addition, the study is also one of the few attempts at the longitudinal observation of the developmental variation of conceptual transfer, which is more advantageous in collecting valid evidence of the conceptual changes caused by L2 learning (Jarvis & Pavlenko 2008: 37).

The generalizability of above findings is, however, impeded by the limited number of participants and their informal L2 learning experience. Only two participants were involved in the study and as revealed in their socio-biographical information, they were members of the working class and English learning was confined to day-to-day contact with the native speakers at work. Therefore, the findings of the study are in need of further examination by conducting large-scale cross-sectional studies in a classroom-based L2 learning setting.

Another problem is that the discussion on the object concept as an underpinning of senses of English spatial prepositions is far from exhaustive. Firstly, the object concept in this study was mainly referred to as the concept of subspaces defined by the reference object, which serves to distinguish the prepositions from each other. For example, what distinguishes *in* from other prepositions is whether location is at an interior subspace or not (Becker & Carroll 1997: 21). However, this can only account for the core senses of prepositions. Aside from this, the physical attributes of the reference objects, like dimensionality or closeness, also play an important part in assigning the semantic values to prepositions. Therefore, a more detailed investigation of the effect of object concept on the use of English spatial prepositions is desired.

Despite these problems, the study well demonstrates the role of object conceptualization in the acquisition of English spatial prepositions and sets a precedent for a conceptual approach to transfer research.

Another brave attempt at interpreting transfer at the conceptual level was made by Zhang and Liu (2013), who conducted a corpus-based study of conceptual transfer in Chinese-speaking learners' use of English prepositions. Different from the above studies, the study paid much attention to the physical attributes of objects in the cross-linguistic comparison. For example, in the form of a schema, the research demonstrated the difference in the attribute of closeness between the reference object required by *in* and that required by *li* (Zhang & Liu 2013). This contributes to a deeper understanding of the cross-linguistic difference in spatial conceptualization and broadens the object concept proposed by Becker and Carroll (1997).

The confirmation of conceptual transfer in the study consisted of a sequence of three steps: (1) Making a comparison in conceptual representation between English prepositions and their Chinese equivalents; (2) Observing the systematic variation in Chinese learners' use of English prepositions in terms of patterns of collocation and colligation; (3) Making a comparison in interlanguage between Chinese-speaking learners and German-speaking learners. Based on the findings, the researchers identified cases of positive and negative conceptual transfer at two levels: Lexical level and grammatical level. The results showed that the cross-linguistic similarities in spatial conceptualization facilitated learners' acquisition of English prepositions and the disparities caused learners to make systematic errors in using prepositions and preposition structures.

Zhang and Liu's study provides explanation for the systematic variation in Chinese-speaking learners' use of English spatial prepositions from the perspective of conceptual transfer and highlights the difference in physical attributes of the reference objects in cross-linguistic comparisons between English spatial prepositions and their Chinese equivalents. However, a big problem with the study is that like the study by Becker and Carroll (1997), the investigation was limited to the prototypical relation of containment and supporting in which the reference object is usually a prototypical container or supporting surface. Actually, similar to semantic categories which consist of prototypical, intermediate and peripheral members (Ma 2007), object categories are also gradient (Ungerer & Schmid 2001). For example, in the following three types of spatial scenes illustrated in Figure 2.12, each of them is categorized as the relation of containment encoded by the preposition *in*:

(43) the pens in the penholder

(44) the foot in the stirrup

(45) the car in the square

But the prototypicality of the containers decreases from left to right. To be precise, of the three containers, the penholder is of the strongest prototypicality by being three-dimensional, deeply concave and bounded. The stirrup is less prototypical with wide openness and the two-dimensional square is in the margin of the CONTAINER category. And to further complicate matters, the square, which is less prototypical than the stirrup, can be categorized as a container in Chinese in some cases, but the stirrup cannot. Such a lack of correspondence between prototypicality and the degrees of cross-linguistic equivalence will cause conceptual transfer not to be as monolithic as what the above studies have presented.

Figure 2.12 Three Types of Spatial Relations Encoded by *in*
(Cuyckens 1993: 48; Ma 2005: 223; Wei 2007: xx)

Another problem with the study is that although the attributes of reference objects required by *in* received some attention, the focus was still on the conceptual representations of the prepositions and their Chinese equivalents, and the fact that the access of relational predicates like spatial prepositions is basically dependent upon how speakers categorize the physical objects they interconnect (Langacker 1987: 215) is still not given due attention. For example, in Figure 2.12, under the influence of L1-based categorization of stirrup, the preposition *on* is more likely to be activated than *in*. Therefore, the scope of investigation should be extended to the conceptual representations of nouns denoting reference objects. This will not only be contributory to revealing the conceptual mechanism of L1 transfer in preposition learning, but also encourage studies of conceptual transfer in acquisition of other relational predicates. Actually, in an earlier study conducted by another two Chinese researchers Li and Cai (2008), they have pointed out that the difference in object conceptualization is one of the sources of conceptual transfer in L2 acquisition of prepositions. However, without making a deep-going discussion, the study failed to arouse wide concern.

To sum up, a lot of achievements have been made in the explorations of the deep-rooted cognitive factors underlying learners' use of English spatial prepositions. More importantly, studies taking a conceptual approach to L1 effect in acquisition of English spatial prepositions emerged. However, as the literature review in the above has shown, there are still some issues needing to be further addressed.

Firstly, while cross-linguistic difference in spatial categorization has been generally proposed as the cognitive mechanism underlying negative transfer in the use of prepositions, central to the studies cited above are the semantic or conceptual representations of prepositions. Given the conceptual dependency of the spatial prepositions on the categorization of reference objects (Langacker 1987), the findings only serve as indirect evidence for the effect of spatial categorization on learners' use of English spatial prepositions. Therefore, an empirical investigation of conceptual transfer from the perspective of categorization of reference objects is needed.

Secondly, in recent transfer studies, there has been a growing recognition that the typological distance across languages is represented not simply as a binary opposition between similarity and dissimilarity but a continuum stretching from full equivalence to zero equivalence (Jarvis 2010; Pavlenko 2009; Ringbom 2007). The different degrees of cross-linguistic equivalence have been found to exert different impacts on L2 learners' performance (Bohnacker & Rosen 2008; Tokowicz & MacWhinney 2005; Trofimovich, et al. 2007) But the classification of language distance is still too broad by using partial equivalence to cover all the intermediate levels falling in between full equivalence and zero equivalence. This will not be helpful for an in-depth exploration of how transfer occurs and changes at different degrees of equivalence, especially for the study of transfer in the acquisition of English spatial prepositions whose semantic contrasts with their Chinese translation equivalents are notoriously complicated.

Based on the above discussion, the researcher, extending the scope of examination from the isolated prepositions to the nouns collocating with them, intends to investigate the conceptual mechanism of L1 transfer in learning of English spatial prepositions from the perspective of categories of reference objects. To this end, a detailed analysis of English-based prototype concept of reference objects and a cross-linguistic comparison in categories of reference objects are made to establish the continuum of prototypicality of reference objects and the continuum of cross-linguistic equivalence in categorization. Besides, the study takes L2 proficiency into consideration to test whether L2 learning will result in a modification of previously acquired L1-based spatial concepts as claimed by Neo-Whorfianism (Pavlenko 2009: 150).

The preposition *in* is chosen as the research focus for the following three reasons: (1) *In* is mainly used as a static preposition and its semantic value is largely dependent on the conceptual representations of nous collocating with it; (2) Previous studies always focused on the comparison between *in* and the Chinese spatial expression *li*, actually *in* is partially equivalent to several Chinese expressions, like *shang*, *xia* or *cong*, but little work has been done in exploring how the spatial concepts represented by these expressions interfere with the acquisition of *in*; (3) Studies on Chinese children's acquisition of spatial expressions reveal that CONTAINMENT is the earliest acquired spatial concept (Kong & Wang 2002; Li, et al. 1992), and simultaneously *in* is also one of the prepositions acquired in the earlier stage of English learning and most frequently used by Chinese learners (Gui 2005), therefore, focusing on *in* will give more insight into the dynamic change of spatial conceptualization with acquisition of a new language.

2.5 Summary

The chapter starts with a prototype approach to categories of reference objects, in which categorization of objects is claimed to involve two dimensions: Intralingual dimension and interlingual dimension. Intralingually speaking, categorization of objects mainly means that speakers within a speech community tend to share in perception of prototypicality of objects as reference points for the location of other objects, which is usually developed in the course of L1 acquisition. However, as to the interlingual dimension, the similarities and differences in judgment of the category membership and typicality of the reference objects across speech communities will be put in the focus of categorization.

Following this is a review of conceptual transfer studies, mainly including the theoretical advances underlying conceptual transfer studies, definition of conceptual transfer and the empirical explorations of conceptual transfer. As shown in the review, conceptual transfer in the domain of space receives increasing attention with the revelation of the language-specific spatial categorization by cross-linguistic studies in Neo-Whorfianism. The final part of the chapter is the review of the achievements that have been made in the empirical studies of the acquisition of English spatial prepositions. Illuminating as they are, two issues are under-explored: (1) How does learners' construal of the conceptual contents of nouns inhibit or facilitate L1 transfer in the use of English spatial prepositions by L2 learners? (2) How do different degrees of cross-linguistic equivalence in categorization exert influence on learners' use of spatial prepositions?

Given these problems, the researcher intends to undertake an empirical study of the effect of categories of reference objects on L2 learners' use of spatial prepositions in hopes of revealing the conceptual mechanism of L1 transfer in the use of such relational predicates as prepositions.

The next chapter provides a detailed account of the theoretical grounds upon which the investigation of how categories of reference objects affect L2 learners' use of English spatial prepositions is conducted to reveal the conceptual mechanism of L1 transfer.

Chapter Three Theoretical Framework

3.1 Introduction

This chapter is devoted to documenting the theoretical underpinnings for the present study, from which the frame of analyzing learners' use of the English spatial preposition *in* is derived. Specifically speaking, the purpose of this chapter is two-fold: (1) Explain how human construal of containers is mapped onto *in*; (2) Reveal the conceptual mechanism of L1 transfer in the use of *in*. To this end, the study firstly draws insights from Langacker's valence relation theory to account for the conceptual dependency of *in* on the construal of containers, and then demonstrates the effect of prototypicality of containers and degrees of cross-linguistic equivalence in the CONTAINER category on the use of *in* by L2 learners within the framework of connectionist approach to bilingual conceptual representation.

3.2 Dependency of the Use of *in* on Categorization of Objects as Containers

In this section, the researcher will initially make a brief introduction of Langacker's valence relation theory (Langacker 1987) and then applies the Analytic Model of Autonomy-dependency Alignment (Niu 2008a, 2008b, 2011) to analyze how a composite preposition structure is formed, through which the dependency of the production of *in* on the CONTAINER category is justified.

3.2.1 Analytic Model of Autonomy-dependency Alignment

The Analytic Model of Autonomy-dependency Alignment was developed by Niu (2008a, 2008b, 2011a, 2011b) on the basis of Langacker's valence relation theory to provide a cognitive account for the formation of grammatical constructions.

In Cognitive Grammar, valence relation was referred to as the "combinatory relationship between component structures" in a grammatical construction (Langacker 1987: 494). With the proposal of valence relation theory, Langacker intended to address the issue of "conceptual combination" between component structures in terms of the establishment of valence relations between them (Taylor 2002: 228). A fundamental assumption of Langacker's valence theory is that a complex structure functioning as a unitary entity is formed via the integration of component structures at a lower level (Langacker 1987: 311). It follows that the construction [IN+N] results from the combination of its two component structures [IN] and [N]. Different from the traditional valence theory which put emphasis on the formal taxonomy in accordance with the number of elements that a linguistic structure, verbs in particular, can govern, Langacker focused on the conceptual nature of combinatory relationship between component structures, which constitutes the cognitive basis of grammatical behavior (Langacker 1987: 277; Niu 2008a: 1). In addition, Langacker rejected the idea of reducing a semantic structure to a bundle of semantic features advocated by the traditional componential analysis and opted for a conceptual approach to the internal structure of the components in combination (Langacker 2002: 3; Niu 2011a: 211).

According to Langacker (1987: 324-326), a valence relation comprises four parts: Correspondence, profile determinacy, conceptual dependency and constituency. Central to it is the conceptual dependency, which serves as a starting point from which the valence relation is established successively (Niu 2011a: 191). As to the conceptual dependency, Langacker (1987: 300) defined it as: "One structure, D, is dependent on the other, A, to the extent that A constitutes an elaboration of a salient schematic substructure within D." Simply put, in a valence relation, a structure is dependent on the other structure in the way that the structure profiles a substructure that is schematic and in need of an elaboration by the other structure. The definition apparently specifies how a structure is judged to be conceptually dependent or autonomous.

To make Langacker's valence theory more operational, Niu (2008a, 2008b, 2011a, 2011b) combined the four parts together and proposed the Analytic Model of Autonomy-dependency Alignment (Figure 3. 1) in an attempt to account for the cognitive mechanism of the formation of a grammatical construction (Niu 2011a: 192).

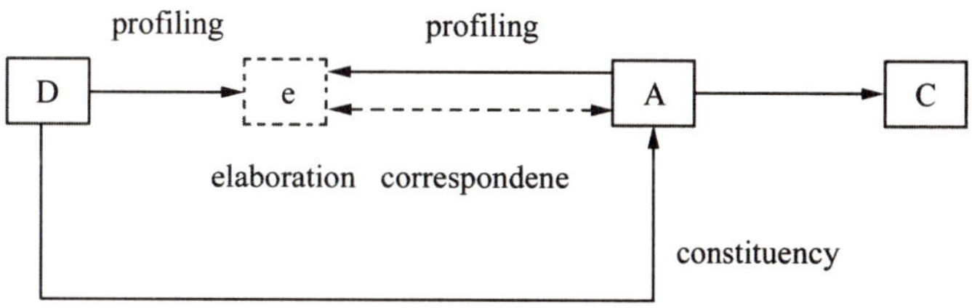

Figure 3. 1 Analytic Model of Autonomy-dependency Alignment (Niu 2011a: 205)

In this model, *D* represents the dependent structure, *A* represents the autonomous structure, *C* represents the constituency, and *e* represents an elaboration site provided by the dependent structure. A dotted box is drawn to emphasize that the structure needing to be elaborated is schematic. The arrows are shown in boldface type to highlight the process of profiling.

Following the model, four important cognitive operations contribute to the establishment of a valence relation. They are profiling, elaboration, correspondence and constituency (Langacker 1987; Niu 2011a).

In Cognitive Grammar, profiling refers to a mental process in which a specific conceptual referent is put in focus by the predicate within a basic conceptual domain (Langacker 1987: 183-188). For example, the three spatial relations shown by Figure 3. 2 are described as "a ball on the box", "a ball in the box" and "a ball under the box" respectively. This indicates that three different referents are profiled by the nominal predicate [BOX]: A supporting surface, a container and a covering. In other words, the conceptual content of the noun *box* is construed as a supporting surface, a container and a covering respectively. Thus, it can be seen that profiling, as a matter of construal, is a process of categorization in which some physical and functional attributes are selectively elevated to a special degree of prominence at the cost of neglecting others and as a result, a specific conceptual referent is evoked. As to the three prepositions, *on*, *in* and *under*, the referent that is made salient is the schematic landmark which calls for specification of the instance profiled by the noun. Such an activity of specification is termed "elaboration" by Langacker (1987).

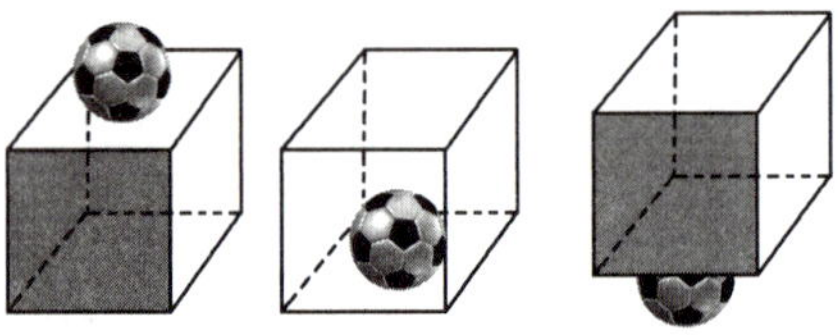

Figure 3.2 The Box in Three Spatial Relations

Elaboration, which is defined as the specification of a schema by its instances (Langacker 1987: 489) is another important cognitive operation that affects the integration between the dependent and autonomous structures. For a substructure profiled by a dependent structure, it exists in the form of a schema which "abstracts the commonalities of a variety of specific instances in a conceptual category" and "lacks in precision and detail" (Langacker 1987: 132), thus it needs to be specified. Langacker termed this a provision of an elaboration site (Langacker 1987: 304). As a response, the autonomous structure will profile a specific object concept to instantiate the schematic category. If the referent evoked is a member of the category, the substructure profiled by the dependent structure will be elaborated. This implies that what a conceptual referent is profiled determines whether the schema can be elaborated or not.

When the schematic substructure is elaborated, the correspondence between the component structures will be established. In chemistry, valence relations between atoms are established on the basis of the overlapping in electrons, as is the integration between the linguistic structures (Langacker 1987: 277). Langacker (1987: 278) speaks of the overlapping as "correspondence". Correspondence occurs as a result of profiling and elaboration and is defined as the basis of the formation of a composite structure (Langacker 1987: 278). In the case of *in the box*, the relational predicate [IN] comprises two important substructures: Landmark and trajector. With the fact that [IN] designates a spatial relation of containment in which a focused object is located inside a region delimited by the reference object, the landmark of [IN] is schematically a thing of concavity, hollowness and boundedness. When the schematically characterized landmark overlaps the profile of the nominal predicate [BOX], or in plain words, when the referent of [BOX] is conceptualized as a container and instantiates the schematic landmark designated by [IN], the integration of the two predicates to form a coherent structure will be permitted (Langacker 1987, 2002).

The final operation Constituency is concerned with the hierarchical organization of grammatical structures. To be precise, component structures are progressively assembled into more and more complex structures (Langacker 1987: 311, 2002: 27). Figure 3.3 sketches the process of the formation of the composite structure [FOOTBALL IN BOX]. [IN] profiles a schematic container and provides an elaboration site. [BOX] profiles an instance of the CONTAIENR category and specifies the schematic container. Then there is the correspondence between the two profiled substructures, permitting the integration between [IN] and [THE-BOX] to result in the composite structure [IN THE BOX], which in turn as a component structure at the next higher level profiles a schematic trajector. As for the nominal predicate [FOOTBAL], it profiles a specific object located in the container and elaborates the schematic trajector. A correspondence is again established between the two profiled substructures. Then [FOOTBALL] and [IN THE BOX] combine to yield a larger composite structure [FOOTBALL IN BOX]. Undoubtedly, constituency at each level presupposes the correspondence between the profiled substructures, which is realized by means of profiling and elaboration.

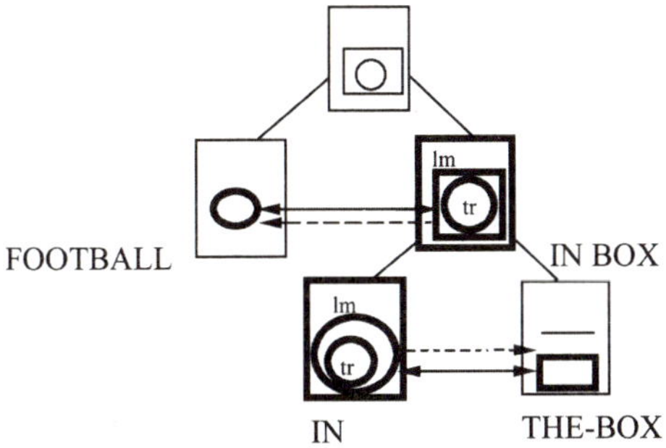

Figure 3.3 Formation of [FOOTBALL IN BOX] (adapted from Langacker 1987: 280)

In the above figure, *lm* and *tr* represent landmark and trajector profiled by [IN] respectively, the bold part represents the operation of profiling, the dotted arrow represents an elaboration site profiled by [IN], the double-headed arrow represents the correspondence between the two profiled substructures and the solid line represents the integration between the component structures. The reason for using a dotted arrow to represent a relation of elaboration is to emphasize that the schematic container is not necessarily elaborated by the profiled substructure of the nominal predicate.

The account of the establishment of a valence relation in terms of the four cognitive operations provides a framework for a bottom-up analysis of the formation of constructions and contributes to unraveling the deep-rooted cognitive mechanism motivating the conceptual integration of the component structures (Niu 2011a).

In the following, the study will apply Niu's (2011a) Analytic Model of Autonomy-dependency Alignment to analyze how a composite preposition structure [IN+N] is formed, through which the cognitive mechanism of the use of *in* will be uncovered.

3.2.2 Formation of the Construction [IN+N]

Two issues need to be handled in the analysis of the formation of a composite preposition structure. The first one is concerned with the confirmation of the dependency of the preposition on the noun and the second one involves a bottom-up analysis of how the two component structures are integrated to form a grammatical construction.

As Langacker (1987: 301-302) has pointed out, whether a structure is conceptually dependent or autonomous is highly correlated with three factors: (1) The salience of a substructure (marked as x_e) within the structure X; (2) The extent to which the structure Y constitutes an elaboration of x_e; (3) The optional access of x_e for Y. This indicates in a spatial relation construction, the dependency of a structure is firstly determined by what substructure is profiled and whether it needs to be elaborated. Following the theory of valence relation, landmark is one of obligatorily accessed substructures for such relational predicates as the prepositions (Langacker 1987: 231, 281). As an abstraction of the commonalities of a variety of specific reference objects, landmark is schematically characterized, lacking precision and details (Langacker 1987: 132). Thus it provides an elaboration site where the nominal predicate instantiates it in finer details by profiling a specific object concept. For instance, in the expression *in the box*, the landmark is specified as a three-dimensional container, whereas in *on the box*, the landmark is an instance of a two-dimensional flat surface. It can be clearly seen that a conceptual referent designated by the noun specifies the category defined by landmark along a variety of parameters (Langacker 1987: 68). In other words, the schematic landmark of the preposition receives great elaboration with the specific properties spelled out by the nominal predicate. Therefore, it is safe to conclude that the preposition is conceptually dependent on the noun predicate.

Aside from this, the dependency relation can be further demonstrated by the fact that in a spatial relation construction dependency is not bidirectional (Langacker 1987: 301). For one thing, the conceptual structure related to the category LANDMAEK is not an obligatorily accessed substructure for the noun (Langacker 1987: 301). Take the ball in Figure 3.2 as an example. The properties defining the ball as a container are selectively ignored both in the first and the third spatial relation where such attributes as "the vertical position of the ball", "the top" and "the bottom" of the ball tend to receive substantial prominence. To put it another way, the object concept is selectively profiled by the noun *ball*. For another thing, landmark profiled by the preposition is schematic relative to the more specific conceptual referents evoked by nouns, each of which elaborates the schematic landmark in finer details in different ways (Langacker 1987: 301). Taken together, in the spatial construction [IN +N], the preposition *in* can be identified as a dependent structure, and the noun as an autonomous structure.

In the following, an analysis of the formation of the specific composite structure [In+N] is undertaken within the framework of the analytic model proposed by Niu (2011a). As reveled in the model, the formation of the structure starts with the profiling of the substructure landmark by the preposition which is the dependent component in the composite structure. The substructure highlighted by *in* is a schematic container, defining the category of containers with features abstracted away from an array of instances, which mainly include closeness, dimensionality and boundedness. The schematic container provides an elaboration site for the autonomous structure, the nominal predicate, which profiles a specific object concept (Langacker 2002: 63). As has been noted above, profiling can be conceived of as a process of categorization in which the referent of the nominal predicate is construed as a specific member of the category defined by the schematic landmark. If the construal of the predicate elaborates the schematic landmark, or, to be more specific; if the referent of the noun is categorized as an instance of CONTAINER, a correspondence will be established between the profiled substructures of the two component structures. As a result, a grammatical composite structure is formed with the conceptual integration of *in* and the nominal predicate. In contrast, if the referent evoked by the noun is not a container, the elaboration site provided by the landmark fails to be instantiated and there is no overlapping between the profiled substructures of the two components. As a result, other prepositions rather than *in* will be accessed to be combined with the noun to form a more complex structure. For instance, at the sight of the following picture, will a speaker describe it as *three apples on the plate* or *three apples in the plate*?

Figure 3.4 Three Apples on the Plate

This is basically dependent on what specific conceptual referent is profiled by the noun *plate*. An analytic model highlighting the process of profiling is sketched to illustrate the formation of the structure [IN+N] on the basis of Niu's model (2011: 205).

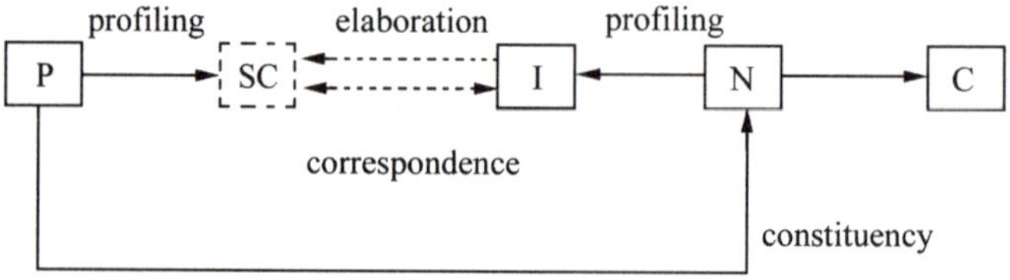

Figure 3.5 Autonomy-dependency Analytic Model for [IN+N]

In this model, *P* stands for the dependent structure [IN], *N* stands for the autonomous structure [N], *SC* stands for the schematic container, and *I* stands for the instance profiled by [N]. Different from Niu's model, this model highlights the instance profiled by the nominal predicate, because it is between the instance and the schematic container that the correspondence is established. *I* is shown in boldface type to emphasize the process of profiling. The dotted arrows are employed to indicate that the instances profiled by the autonomous structure are not necessarily the ones corresponding with the elaboration site provided by a given preposition. In Figure 3.2, the same object is put into three categories, elaborating three types of landmark profiled by the preposition *under*, *in* and *on* respectively. This implies that the use of *in* is conceptually dependent on whether the instance profiled by the nominal predicate elaborates the schematic container. According to Langacker (1987: 69), the degree to which the schema is elaborated by its instantiation is named as elaborative distance. Then how far is it between the instance and the schematic substructure? Where will they meet to arrive at a correspondence? The answer will be found in the two modes of categorization proposed by Langacker.

According to Langacker (1987: 371), there are two modes of categorization: Categorization by schemas and categorization by prototypes. By the first mode of categorization, the specification of the schematic characterization of a given category by an instance is emphasized. For instance, in Examples (43)(45), the three nouns *penholder*, *stirrup* and *square* instantiate the schematic container profiled by the preposition *in*. As regards the second mode of categorization, it is primarily concerned with the category membership on the basis of perceived similarity with prototype. Thus, within this mode of categorization, the containers denoted by the three nouns are of different degrees of prototypicality in terms of the number of the attributes they share with a typical container.

Langacker pointed out both of the two modes of categorization "reside in a comparison event of the form S>T=V" (1987: 371). *S* stands for "standard" and it can be recognized as a schema or a prototype. *T* refers to the object to be categorized and *V* means the value of discrepancy between the standard and the target, which is dependent on how well the target resembles the prototype as a result of the viewer's comparison (1987: 371). To be precise, if the target resembles prototype to the extent of a full specification of the schematic characterization, the value of discrepancy will be zero, whereas if the target is deviant from the prototype in one or more than one attribute, the schema is partially specified and thus, *V* has a nonzero value (1987: 371). It, then, follows that the elaborative distance between the schematic container and the instance is determined by how well the object to be categorized resembles the prototype, or in other words, the elaborative distance is dependent on the prototypicality of the instance in accordance with the prototype approach to categorization (Rosch 1978; Ungerer & Schmid 2001). Concerning the formation of the construction [IN+N], the elaborative distance between the schematic container profiled by the preposition *in* and an instance profiled by the noun is defined by the prototypicality of the instance as a container denoted by the noun. The more prototypical the instance is, the smaller the elaborative distance is. Then, there will be greater possibility of forming a composite structure headed by *in*. Based on the above discussion, the analytic model accounting for the formation of the structure [IN + N] can be further specified as follows:

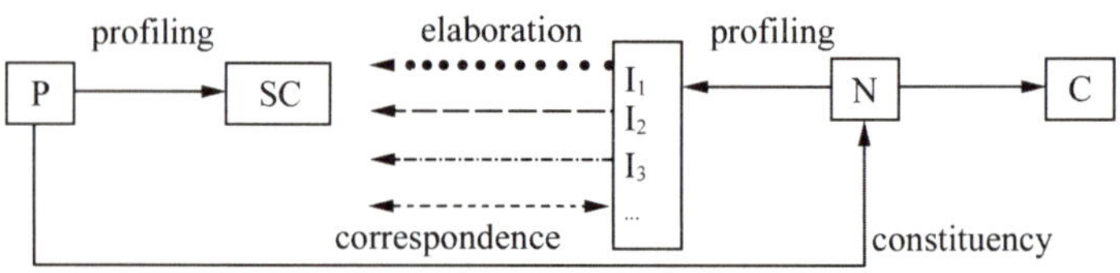

Figure 3. 6 Autonomy-dependency Analytic Model Involving Prototypicality

In this model, I_n stands for the instances of CONTAINER profiled by the nominal predicates, which are of different degrees of prototypicality. The dashed-line arrows are made boldfaced to various degrees to indicate different elaborative distances. As prototypicality of the instance declines, the distance between the schema and the specific instance is increasing. As noted in Section 2. 2. 2, within a speech community, construal of reference objects mainly refers to L1-based perception of prototypicality of objects as reference points for the location of other objects, which is usually developed in the course of L1 acquisition. Neo-Whorfianism (Slobin 1996) also argued that the L1 one learns as a child affects his categorization of the world. This suggests that monolingual English natives will on the basis of their L1 experience develop English-based prototype concept which determines the elaborative distance between the schematic container and the instance evoked by the noun. Thus, it might be reasonably assumed that English-based prototype concept constitutes an important cognitive mechanism of the use of *in* by English natives. But as to L2 learners of English who have experience in more than one language, what might determine the elaborative distance and in turn underlie their use of *in*? In Section 2.2.2, it is also stated that construal of reference objects across speech communities involves the similarities and dissimilarities in judging the category membership and typicality of the reference objects. Then, do the similarities and dissimilarities exert any influence on learners' use of *in*? In the following, the researcher will probe deeply into the cognitive mechanism of the use of *in* by L2 learners based on the connectionist approach to bilingual conceptual representation.

3.3 Cognitive Basis of the Use of *in* by Second Language Learners

Neo-Whorfianism has pointed out that language acquisition not only involves the acquisition of language forms but concepts represented by the forms, as Slobin (1996: 91) put it:

> The Language or languages that we learn in childhood are not neutral coding systems of an objective reality. Rather each one is a subjective orientation to the world of human experience, and this orientation affects the ways in which we think while we are speaking.

It follows, then, that what underlies the use of *in* by a monolingual English native is L1-based categories of reference objects, which are developed in the course of L1 acquisition (Bowerman 2007). Then what is the cognitive basis of the use of *in* by learners of English as a L2?

In this section, the researcher will delve into the issue on the basis of connectionist approach to bilingual mental representation and then attempt to design an analytic model explaining the process of the formation of composite structures peculiar to second language learners.

3.3.1 Connectionist Approach to Bilingual Conceptual Representation

In psycholinguistic studies of bilingualism, one of the most controversial questions is whether bilinguals, with acquisition of L2 coding system, have a single conceptual system shared by the two languages or separate systems accessed by each language (Kroll & Tokowicz 2005: 531).

Early research on the issue was conducted under the influence of symbolic accounts of knowledge representation which assumed that language knowledge is stored as a highly structured system of symbols (Gong & Guo 2010: 58; Hulstijn 2002: 196), and got trapped in the opposition between distinct meaning models and common meaning models (Finkbeiner 2002: 13). The former claimed that with acquisition of L2 forms, a new L2-based conceptual representation is developed correspondingly (Finkbeiner 2002: 14). This indicates that at the sight of the color, Chinese-speaking learners of English will activate two isolated concepts of the color that are associated with the Chinese form *hong* and the English form *red* respectively. In stark contrast to this view, the common meaning models argued against the addition of a new conceptual system and assumed that interlingual equivalents share a common conceptual representation, but the strength of the link between the concept and the two forms is different and changeable with the development of second language competence (Finkbeiner 2002: 15). A series of empirical tests focusing on the cross-language semantic priming effects between translation equivalents reveal that neither of the two models is fully justified (Kroll & Tokowicz 2005: 531).

Ever since the 1990s, as connectionist approach to knowledge representation made significant inroads into mainstream cognitive psychology, connectionism-based distributed models of bilingual mental representation emerge as solutions to the above problem (de Groot 1992; Dong & Gui 2002; Finkbeiner 2002; Li 2006; Pavlenko 2009) with attention shifted to the internal structure of conceptual representation (Pavlenko 2009: 125). Different from symbolism, connectionism assumes that knowledge is distributed over many processing units and connections rather than stored as individual entities at specific addresses (Haberlandt 1994: 189-190; Li 2006: 321). Take the conceptual representations of the Chinese form *hong* as an example. For a

Chinese native speaker, the concept that *hong* activates is not represented as a single independent unit comprising a structured system of conceptual features or nodes, but as a pattern of activation of the relevant conceptual features (Li 2006: 321). The same holds true for its English equivalent *red*. But their distributed representations are different. As demonstrated by Figure 3. 7, the conceptual primitives associated with generic attributes usually remain at the same level of activation, but the ones related to culture-specific experience have different activation levels.

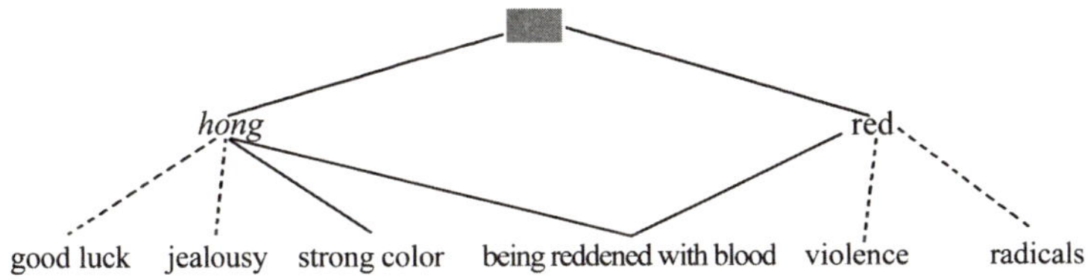

Figure 3. 7 Conceptual Representations of *hong* and *red*

For example, in the expression *hong yan bing*, the feature [jealousy] will be at a high level of activation in the conceptual representations of *hong*, but as we switch to English, [jealousy] will be inhibited.

Another important claim made by connectionism is that new language learning experience will modify and change previously built connection weights between the units that are specific to L1 (Haberlandt 1994; Li 2006; Wang 2001). With accumulation of such language experience as "*kai men hong*", "*hong yun dang tou*" or "*ben ming nian zha hong yao dai*", the link between *hong* and the primitive [good luck] is reinforced repeatedly and this results in a high activation level of [good luck]. However, as learners are exposed to the English expressions with the word *red* (e. g. , *a red rag to a bull*, or *see red*), the connection between the primitive [violence] and *red* will be strengthened and the activation pattern will be restructured accordingly.

Under the influence of connectionist accounts of language representation and acquisition, there emerged an array of distributed models of bilingual mental representation (de Groot 1992; Dong & Gui 2002; Finkbeiner 2002; Li 2006; Pavlenko 2009) which held that conceptual representations should be comprised of a distributed set of conceptual features or nodes (Finkbeiner 2002: 16). Central to these models is the analysis of what conceptual features are shared and what are language-specific and how the pattern of distribution is modified with accumulation of L2 learning experience (Pavlenko 2009: 126).

Of the distributed models, Sense Model proposed by Finkbeiner (2002) is a highly influential one. What distinguishes it from other models is that it argued for the representational asymmetry between the translation equivalents in terms of the number of conceptual features that are activated by forms. As the model claimed, the representational asymmetry between the translation equivalents is mainly manifested in the following two aspects (Finkbeiner 2002: 153):

(1) More conceptual features are represented by L1 forms than their L2 translation equivalents (Figure 3.8), to put it simply, the number of features that is linked with L1 forms is larger than that linked with L2 forms;

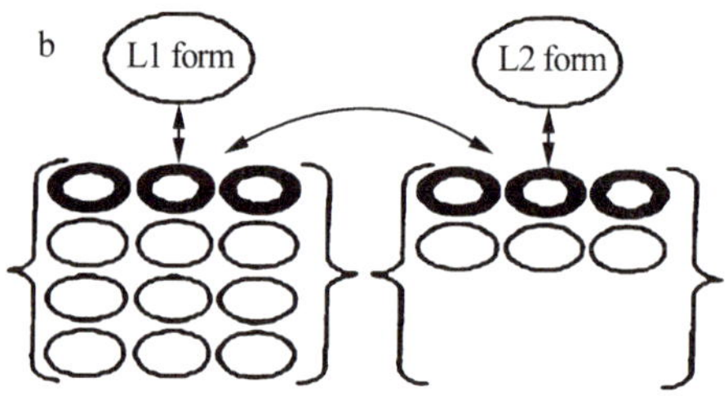

Figure 3.8 Sense Model (Finkbeiner 2002: 17)

(2) L2 forms tend to activate more L1-based conceptual features rather than L2-based ones, as a result, the conceptual structure underlying the use of a L2 form mainly consists of the L1-based conceptual features.

Then between the two translation equivalents *hong* and *red*, there are fewer conceptual features that are represented by *red* than those represented by *hong* in the conceptual store of a Chinese-speaking English learner. And furthermore, while *red* is used by the learner, the features that are linked with *hong* mostly remain at a high level of activation and few features specific to *red* are activated. This implies that if the two translation equivalents fully overlap in the pattern of activation, there will be positive influence from L1, or else, negative transfer will occur. For example, Chinese learners of English might say *red-eyed* instead of *green-eyed* to mean jealousy. However, with the adaptation of connection weights between concept and form under the reinforcement of L2 learning experience, more L2-specific conceptual features are activated and the cross-linguistic difference in conceptual representations is gradually recognized by learners. As a result, the L2 form-concept mapping will be established to resist the interference from L1.

With implications drawn from the distributed models, an attempt is made to analyze the cognitive underpinning of the use of *in* by Chinese learners of English in hopes of revealing the conceptual mechanism of L1 transfer.

3.3.2 Conceptual Mechanism of L1 Transfer in the Use of *in* by L2 Learners

As discussed above, the use of *in* is largely determined by whether or not the schematic landmark profiled by *in* can be elaborated by the object concept profiled by the nominal predicate. As far as monolingual English natives are concerned, prototypicality-based categorization developed in the course of L1 acquisition constitutes an important mechanism of the use of *in*. However, as to the bilingual speakers, who have a command of two interrelated modes of categorization, what underlies their use of *in*?

According to the distributed class of models, the concept profiled by the nominal predicate is manifested as a pattern of activation formed on the basis of language experience (Finkbeiner 2002). The frequent exposure to the expression *pan zi li* will cause the features relevant to the CONTAINER category to be at a high level of activation and result in the construal of *pan zi* as a container. However, in English, the conventional combination between *plate* and *on* will lead to the activation of features defining the category of SUPPORTING SURFACE. Then, for a Chinese-speaking English learner, his conceptualization of the object will comprise two patterns of activation. As he switches to L2, the features related to the CONTAINER category will be inhibited and the ones related to the category of SUPPORTING SURFACE will be activated. This implies that a successful switch from L1 to L2 is based on a successful activation of L2-specific features (MacWhinney 2007).

However, for the learners with insufficient L2 learning experience, there will be representational asymmetry between the translation equivalents (Finkbeiner 2002). Specifically speaking, with a lack of L2 input, the conceptual representations are dominated by the L1-based features and the direct linkage between the English noun and L2-specific features has not yet been well established. Therefore, what the noun activates is mostly L1-based conceptual features borrowed from its L1 equivalent. This suggests that the conceptual features linked with L1 equivalent are liable to remain at the same level of activation while speaking English. Thus if the translation equivalents are fully equivalent in the pattern of activation, the object will be put into the same category and cause the schematic landmark required by the English preposition to be elaborated. But what will happen if they are partially equivalent or not equivalent?

Take the noun *square* and its Chinese equivalent *guang chang* as an example. Given the fact that both of them can be combined with the expressions encoding the relation of containment, they both can profile the object concept specifying the schematic container. But *guang chang* can also combine with *shang*, and furthermore, the combination is more frequent than that with *li*. An implication is that the features relevant to the CONTAINER category are not as strongly linked with *guang chang* as the ones defining the category of SUPPORTING SURFACE. Therefore, at the early stage of L2 learning, what *square* activates tends to be the features that have an easier access to *guang chang* and as a result, the square is categorized as a supporting surface which elaborates the schematic landmark profiled by *on*. But since there is also some linkage between the CONTAINER category and *guang chang*, which suggests that the conceptual representations have contained some features relevant to CONTAINER, *in* is also likely to be accessed such that the occurrence of negative transfer is inhibited to some extent.

Concerning the forms that are not equivalent in spatial conceptualization, the possibility for the negative transfer might be increased. Just as noted above, *pan zi* and *plate* are connected with the categories of CONTIANER and SURFACE respectively. Then the correct use of English spatial prepositions calls for an inhibition of features specific to L1. But with a lack of L2 input, what the noun activates is mostly L1-based conceptual features. Since the features relevant to SURFACE are not present in L1-based conceptual representations, there is little chance for the features to be activated, and therefore, the schematic landmark profiled by the preposition *on* is hardly elaborated. In this case, the potential for negative transfer from the L1 is the strongest. Only when L2-based pattern of activation is formed and repeatedly reinforced by an increasing exposure to the expression *on the plate*, can learners come to realize the specifications of L2 lexical concepts that are divergent from L1 (Finkbeiner 2002).

From the foregoing analysis, it can be seen that at the initial stage of L2 learning, language distance in categorization tends to impose more constraints on the use of *in* by bilingual learners than prototypicality of containers. If L1-based categorization is fully equivalent to the L2, the referent of L2 form will be construed in the same way that the referent of its L1 equivalent is construed. As a result, the schematic landmark profiled by *in* is elaborated and *in* is correctly used. As degrees of equivalence declines, fewer L2-specific features are activated and the possibility for the schematic container to be elaborated is reduced. This facilitates the occurrence of negative transfer. Therefore, it might be reasonably assumed that the variation in cross-linguistic equivalence in categorization defines the elaborative distance between the schematic container and the object concept profiled by the noun and constitutes an important mechanism of L1 transfer in the use of *in*.

Following connectionist accounts of L2 learning (Ellis 2011, 2013; Wang 2001) which highlight that the frequency with which learners are exposed to a specific structure is a function of association of conceptual features, a high frequency of the combination between the preposition *in* and the nouns referring to the containers of high prototypicality is contributory to strengthening the connection weights of the features defining the CONTAINER category. Then, with an increasing exposure to L2 input, bilingual speakers might gradually develop a prototypicality-based categorization like native speakers. This suggests that the elaborative distance between the targeted object and the schematic landmark will be put under the influence of both prototypicality and degrees of cross-linguistic equivalence. Therefore, the formation of the composite structure [IN+N] can be sketched as follows:

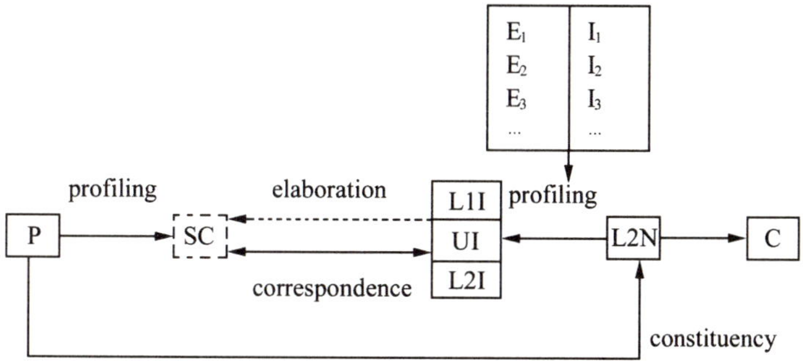

Figure 3.9 Autonomy-dependency Analytic Model for the Formation of [IN+N] by L2 Learners

In this model, *L1I* stands for L1-specific instance, *L2I* stands for L2-specific instance, *UI* stands for the instance shared by the two languages and E_n stands for degrees of equivalence are the CONTAINER category between English and Chinese. If degrees of equivalence are more powerful in defining the elaborative distance, what instance will be profiled depends on degrees of equivalence. In the case of lower degrees of equivalence, L1-specific instances are profiled to elaborate the schematic landmark profiled by other prepositions and interfere with the access of *in*, whereas in the case of higher degrees of equivalence, the object concept represented by both L2 nouns and their L1 equivalents is a container specifying the schematic landmark profiled by *in* and facilitates the use of *in* by learners. If English-based prototypicality is more influential, L2-specific instances are profiled to elaborate the schematic container and *in* will be used in the native-like manner by L2 learners.

In accordance with the connectionist approach to the dynamic development of bilingual conceptual representations, it might be hypothesized that the use of *in* by L2 learners is firstly conceptually motivated by degrees of cross-linguistic equivalence which constitute the conceptual mechanism of L1 transfer in the use of *in* by L2 learners of English. As exposure to L2 input increases, prototypicality-based categorization will also be an important cognitive mechanism of the use of *in*.

To test the hypothesis, an empirical investigation of the effects of prototypicality of containers and degrees of cross-linguistic equivalence in categorization of containers on Chinese learners' use of *in* is conducted. But before it, a preliminary study is done to address the following two questions: (1) What is English-based prototypicality of containers in English? (2) What are the degrees of equivalence in categorization of containers between English and Chinese?

The study consists of two parts. The first, based on previous studies, focuses on the classification of containers in terms of prototypicality related to different uses of *in*. In the second part, a corpus-based cross-linguistic comparison of the CONTAINER category between English and Chinese is made in an attempt to divide the equivalence into different degrees ranging from full equivalence to zero equivalence.

3.4 Summary

In this chapter, much effort is devoted to arguing over the dependency of the use of *in* on the construal of containers within the framework of cognitive grammar and connectionist approach to bilingual conceptual representations, on the basis of which the conceptual mechanism of L1 transfer in the use of English spatial prepositions is brought to light. Firstly, drawing on Langacker's (1987) valence theory and Niu's (2011) Analytic Model of Autonomy-dependency Alignment, the researcher analyzes the process of forming the grammatical construction [IN + N] and demonstrates that the use of *in* is conceptually dependent on the construal of the nominal predicate. Following this is the justification of the effect of degrees of cross-linguistic equivalence in categorization on the use of *in* by English learners on the basis of connectionist accounts of bilingual conceptual representations. After that, an analytical model accounting for the formation of the preposition structure [IN + N] by L2 learners is established. As revealed in the model, degrees of cross-linguistic equivalence in the CONTAINER category constitute the mechanism of L1 transfer in the use of *in*, but as English learning experience accumulates, there will be an increasing involvement of English-based prototype effect which leads to a reduction of negative L1 conceptual transfer.

The next chapter is concerned with a preliminary study of English-based prototype concept of CONTAINER and degrees of cross-linguistic equivalence in CONTAINER between English and Chinese, on the basis of which an empirical investigation of the effects of prototypicality of containers and the degrees of equivalence in categorization on the use of *in* by L2 learners is to be made.

Chapter Four Categorization of Containers—A Preliminary Study

4.1 Introduction

The English spatial preposition *in* is a lexical device decoding a relation of containment in which an object is located at an interior space delimited by the reference object (Becker & Carroll 1997: 21). The landmark profiled by *in* is a schematic container which provides an abstract characterization of the geometrical and functional properties for the identification of different possible reference objects as members of the CONTAINER category. The reference objects existing in various shapes are categorized as containers on the basis of family resemblance which is established by means of mental manipulations of object concepts. They elaborate the schematic container along a variety of topological parameters, mainly including dimensionality, boundedness and hollowness. Intralingually, the reference objects construed as containers are included in the category to various extents because their membership is not an absolute but a gradient phenomenon (Zelinsky-Wibbelt 1993: 4). In accordance with their resemblance to the prototype, they can be differentiated along a continuum of typicality. Interlingually, on the one hand, the universal cognitive mechanism and similar culture experience facilitate the development of categorization universal to languages, and on the other hand, culture-specific experience orients speakers to attend different dimensions of the world and gives birth to disparities in categorization.

This chapter starts with a classification of prototypicality of containers as related to different uses of *in* on the basis of previous studies, and then a corpus-based cross-linguistic comparison of the CONTAINER category between English and Chinese is made.

4.2 Prototypicality of Containers

The identification of prototypicality of containers is mainly based on the work by Hottenroth (1993) and Cuyckens (1993), both of which, unlike other studies limited to the semantic categories of *in* (Herskovits 1986; Vandeloise 1994; Tyler & Evans 2003), were dedicated to characterizing the internal structure of the CONTAINER category, unraveling the cognitive basis of the semantic values of *in*.

4.2.1 Hottenroth's and Cuyckens' Studies on Prototypicality of Containers

In the studies of spatial semantics of prepositions within the paradigm of cognitive linguistics, much effort is dedicated to characterizing the semantic category of the preposition *in* in the form of bundles of conceptual primitives (Hersovits 1986; Lindstromberg 1997; Ma 2007; Tyler & Evans 2003; Vandeloise 1994). For example, Ma delineated the typical sense of *in* as follows:

[containment+full enclosure+full occluding]

As mentioned above, the semantic values are assigned by categorization of objects, especially categorization of objects serving as reference points (Langacker 1987). Therefore, focusing on the combination of primitives to the neglect of how containers are categorized fails to reveal the cognitive basis of the use of *in*. In view of this, some researchers shifted the focus to the categories of reference objects in an attempt to explore the cognitive basis of the access of *in* (Aurnague, et al. 2007; Cuyckens 1993; Hottenroth 1993; Zhang & Liu 2008).

Highly influential in the research on prototypicality of containers are the two studies by Hottenroth (1993) and Cuyckens (1993).

Hottenroth (1993) centered on the diverse senses of the French spatial preposition *dans* which is the equivalent of English spatial preposition *in* and made a revelation of the cognitive principles contributing to the establishment of family resemblance across category members. The principles mainly include mental creation of boundaries and conceptual projection across domains by which the objects in various sizes and shapes are subsumed under the CONTAINER category. Centering around the three parameters related to the typological properties of a container: "dimensionality", "hollowness" (whether the inside of the reference object is materially occupied) and "boundedness", Hottenroth (1993: 214-215) classified the containers into eight types in descending order of prototypicality. Similar ideas were found in Cuyckens' research (1993) on the Dutch equivalent *in*, in which the researcher claimed explicitly that what distinguishes *in* from other prepositions is the spatial characteristics of the reference object where the spatial senses of prepositions hinge (Cuyckens 1993: 36-37). Like Hottenroth, Cuyckens (1993) also advocated "dimensionality", "boundedness" and "hollowness" as three important attributes defining a container. Containers that are three-dimensional, bounded in space and hollow inside tend to be treated as prototypical members of the category. The intermediate and peripheral members diverge from the prototype with missing of one or more attributes. But they are somehow related to each other through the similarity in at least one attribute.

Drawing on the above two studies, the present research attempts to take a geometric-functional approach to the categorization of the objects as specifications of the schematic landmark profiled by *in* along the dimension of prototypicality. Two improvements are made in the study. Firstly, considering that the attribute "boundedness" proposed by Hottenroth and Cuyckens is meant to highlight the closeness of the object to the exclusion of the attribute "discreteness", which is also an important property to differentiate containers, the study splits "boundedness" into "closeness" and "discreteness". "Closeness" mainly stands in contrast with "openness" which stresses whether the objects are materially bounded in all sides or partially bounded. "Discreteness" is proposed to make a distinction between the count object and the mass object. The former is composed of discrete subparts and is objectively bounded in space, whereas the latter tends to be treated as an undifferentiated whole extending indefinitely in space (Vandeloise 2007: 37-43). The linguistic instantiation is the division between count nouns and mass nouns (Langacker 1987: 203). Secondly, the functional nature of each type of containers is also discussed in detail in the present descriptive framework. As is noted above, most of our cognitive operations in conceptualization of objects are functionally motivated; therefore, descriptions of functional interactions between the reference object and the located object will be contributory to revealing how the different types of reference objects are integrated to a systematic category.

4.2.2 Classification of Containers in Terms of Prototypicality

An analysis of the instances of CONTAINER related to the different uses of *in* reveals that there are altogether seven types of containers in terms of prototypicality as demonstrated in Table 4.1. In the following, a detailed description for each instance is offered. Unless otherwise stated, the examples provided are from British National Corpus (BNC).

Table 4.1 ***Prototypicality of Containers***

	Dimensionality	Hollowness	Closeness	Discreteness
I	three	hollow	fully close	discrete, bounded
II	three	hollow	partially close	discrete, bounded
III	three	solid	fully close	discrete, bounded
IV	three	hollow/solid	—	indiscrete, vaguely bounded or unbounded
V	two	—	—	discrete, bounded
VI	two	—	—	indiscrete, vaguely bounded or unbounded
VII	two	—	—	—

The first type of containers (Type I) is characterized as being three-dimensional, hollow, fully enclosed and materially bounded in space. With a hollow region completely enclosed by the internal layer, the containers within this category are primarily used to prevent the located objects from moving outside, and secondarily to protect the located objects from being discovered or accessed. This type of containers constitutes the best example of the

CONTAINER category and provides a full specification of the schematic container profiled by *in*.

This suggests that there is the greatest possibility of the combination between the preposition *in* and the nouns referring to the objects of this type, as in Examples (46)-(48):

(46) They locked her in the car.

(47) My car and house keys were in the bag.

(48) He left his personal belongs in the room.

It can be observed that despite great variation in size, all are put into the CONTAINER category by means of topological characterization (Talmy 2000) as mentioned in Section 2. 2. 1.

However, a point worthy of mention is that not all the objects of this type will be construed as containers. This takes us back to Figure 2. 6.

With a boundary provided by a supporting surface, the bowl constitutes a full enclosure for the pear. However, the function of the enclosure mainly resides in concealing, rather than in controlling the movement of the pear. This indicates that the functional zone of the reference object is not the hollow inside, but the reversed bottom, or in other words, the bottom of the bowl contributes more to the interaction between the bowl and the pear. Motivated by this functional experience, the reference object will be more likely to be construed as a two-dimensional surface higher than the located object. Then the landmark receiving elaboration is the one profiled by the spatial preposition *under* rather than *in*.

The second type of containers (Type II) is connected with the best example by overlapping in "dimensionality", "hollowness" and "discreteness", but they deviate from the best example in the degree of closeness. More precisely, all the reference objects are featured with not enclosing in all sides and exhibiting various continua of partial openness (Hottenroth 1993: 195), as illustrated below:

(49) He put a little of the red liquid in the glass.

(50) They are often expected to spend days on the march, even sleeping in the saddle.

(51) Put your left foot in the stirrup.

It shows that such an instance of containers can be the objects extending inward deeply and leaving one side open (e. g., the glass), or the ones extending inward slightly (e. g., the saddle), or the ones leaving more than one side open (e. g., stirrup) (Hottenroth 1993). With the loss of the attribute "full closeness", the objects of this type are deprived of the protective function, but the function of constraining the movement of the located object within a bounded region is retained. Similar to Type I, the physical force to control the movement is from the boundaries in all directions. But the variation in the degree of closeness motivates the mental closure of a hollow region in different ways (Hottenroth 1993: 196). Since the closure is created mentally, the viewers can choose to impose boundaries on the object concept or not. Such a choice of course is not arbitrary, but largely language-mediated. As Slobin (1996: 107) argued, language being used often favors particular perspectives. With the expression *foot in the stirrup*, English sets the functional zone within an interior bounded by the material object itself and "imaginary planes through its sides" (Cuyckens 1993: 46) whereby the reference object stirrup is conceptualized as a container with a mental completion of a closure, whereas in Chinese, the part of the object that exercises control over the located object is reduced to the bottom of the stirrup and other sides are selectively ignored. As a result, the reference object is construed as a supporting surface with no mental creation of a closure, hence "*ma deng shang de jiao*". This suggests that between English and Chinese, there usually exists cross-linguistic diversity in construal of Type II containers.

The third type of containers (Type III) moves farther away from the best example with the loss of the attribute "hollowness", but with the preservation of other defining attributes and the function of location control, they can still be categorized as containers by conceptual projection from the domain of hollowness to that of solidness. The objects featuring this type of containers are usually "solid chunks of material" (Cuyckens 1993: 50). Here are some examples:

(52) A rough towel hangs from a nail <u>in the wall</u> above the basin.

(53) There is a tiny crack <u>in the ice</u>.

(54) He noticed a hole <u>in the ground</u>.

Different from the above two types of containers, the interior where the reference object and the located object interact is not hollow but "occupied by the material of the reference object" (Hottenroth 1993: 197). The difference can be illustrated by Examples (55)-(56):

(55) the apple in the bowl

(56) the crack in the bowl

In the first case, the apple which is located in a hollow interior walled by the inner boundary of the bowl and an imaginary boundary remains a separate object inside the bowl. But for the second one, by being embedded in the solid chunk of material of the bowl, the crack seems to be a part of the reference object. Therefore, some researchers also identify the location relation between Type III containers and located objects as a part-whole relation (Cuyckens 1993; Ma 2007). Similar to Type II containers, there is also cross-linguistic difference between English and Chinese which is also attributed to the culture-specific perspectives from which the world is viewed. In Chinese, a static embedding relation as mentioned above is often construed as a supporting relation encoded by the Chinese locative marker *shang* which is equivalent to the preposition *on*. This indicates that Chinese speakers tend to construe the reference objects of this type as a two-dimensional supporting surface which is a schematic landmark profiled by *on* rather than *in*.

The fourth type of containers (Type IV) refers to a group of three-dimensional objects that are not discrete individuals, but undifferentiated wholes. Objects featuring this type of containers include mass material objects (e. g., water), natural phenomena (e. g., light or rain) and space portions (e. g., heaven), all of which were named as "mass objects" by Langacker (1987: 205). For instance,

(57) You could see the fish in the water.

(58) I could only see his eyes shining in the light.

(59) He is just standing there in the rain.

According to Langacker (1987: 205), the mass objects are featured with "homogeneity" in the sense that they can be divided without losing their identity; in other words, the subparts of a mass object are not as identifiable as a count object. Given a volume of air in a bottle, no matter how many subparts it is divided into, it is still identified as air. But for a count object (e. g., a box), disassembling it into its components, the top, bottom or flanks, will make it no longer recognized as a box. Therefore, dissimilar to the above three types of reference objects whose functional zones can be reduced to the individual subparts, Type IV containers fulfill the function of location as a whole. Another important feature of mass objects is their unlimited expansion in all directions, which causes them to be likely to be conceived of as a kind of environment surrounding the located object. In this case, the located object is usually much smaller and stays or moves within the reference object. One point worth mentioning is that in some languages like Chinese, if the reference object is light in various forms (e. g., sunlight or moonlight), the force of controlling is usually perceived as coming from above, and therefore, light will not be construed as a container but a protector or controller high above the located object, which instantiates the schematic landmark profiled by the locative expression *xia*, the equivalent of *under*.

By far, the instances of the CONTAINER category identified mainly deviate from the prototype in the specifications of hollowness, closeness and discreteness. Indeed, they may also vary along the parameter of dimensionality (Cuyckens 1993: 52). With the conceptual projection from the three-dimensional configurations onto the two-dimensional and one-dimensional configurations, the two-dimensional and one-dimensional objects may also be construed as members of the CONTAINER category.

Both the fifth (Type V) and sixth (Type VI) type of containers are two-dimensional, but they differ in "discreteness". As to Type V, the reference objects are featured with clear boundaries that distinguish them from the rest of the surrounding area or environment (Cuyckens 1993: 52). This constitutes an important geometrical attribute that makes it possible to be categorized as containers. Here are the instances of the two-dimensional and discrete containers:

(60) Write your name in the margin.

(61) She parked her car in the square.

(62) He was standing in the shade.

The reference objects of this type are usually bounded by a one-dimensional line, but the line is not part of the functional zone of containers

(Cuyckens 1993: 53). Actually if the focus is set on the boundary line, the object will be put into a different category. For example,

(63) a car waiting on the edge of the square

It can be seen in Example (63) that as the functional zone moves to the edge of the square, the spatial relation between the car and the square is construed as a relation of supporting.

In comparison with three-dimensional objects, two-dimensional objects, well-delineated as they are, tend to alternate between CONTAINER and SUPPORTING SURFACE in accordance with the perspectives taken by the viewers. If viewers pay more attention to the vertical orientation and the supporting function, the reference object will be construed as a supporting surface rather than a container. With the schematic landmark profiled by the preposition *on* being elaborated, *on* is accessed to form a prepositional construction. For example,

(64) the cow in the field (Ma 2007)

(65) the players on the field

In Example (64), the use of *in* indicates that the noun *field* is construed as a bounded area in which the cow is located or moves around. However, in Example (65), with focus shifted to the supporting function of the field, *field* is conceptualized as a piece of land on which the players run, jump or kick in a ball game. As a result, the schematic landmark profiled by *on* is elaborated and *on* is activated.

By being unbounded, Type VI containers are close to the margin of the category. However, motivated by visual and functional experience, categorizing the unbounded two-dimensional objects as instances of the CONTAINER category is still possible. For example,

(66) Moses finds a shepherd in the desert.

(67) There wasn't a star to be seen in the sky.

(68) It accounts for roughly seven percent of all beer sales in the continent.

The conceptualization of a desert as a container might be attributed to its configuration. Specifically speaking, although like a plateau or a prairie, a desert also refers to a landform extending unboundedly, it is not as flat as the plateau or prairie and is simultaneously filled with sags and crests. In addition, the fact that a desert is traditionally perceived to be covered with sand and that the feet of creatures standing or moving in the desert are always sunk in sand might also be a prerequisite for a desert to be construed as a container.

The motivation for the sky to be identified as a container might be found in the etymology of the word *sky*. According to the online etymology dictionary (www. etymonline. com), *ky* derives from Proto-Indo-Etymology root *keu-* which means "to hide, to conceal" and *sky* in old English means "clouds" or "heaven". This suggests that sky is originally conceptualized as an area within which the bird, the plane and the like move about safely.

The last type of containers (Type VII) is situated at the boundary of the category. As the most peripheral member, the reference objects within this group are rare (Hottenroth 1993: 202). They mostly exist in the form of "collections" (Vandeloise 2007: 42), and the located object as a member of the collection is spatially close to other members and moves within the area delimited by the collection. It seems that the location relation between this type of containers and located objects can also be identified as a part-whole relation. The functionally motivated conceptual projection from the three-dimensional configuration onto the one-dimensional configuration is a necessary mental operation for the few one-dimensional objects to be categorized as containers. For instance,

(69) The last <u>in the line</u> was the fair woman.

(70) I was second <u>in the queue</u>.

(71) I had seen his name in the list of members of the Society.

With the manipulation of mental closure and conceptual projection, the line or the queue is categorized as a container. One point to bear in mind is that in the region defined by the reference object, the continuity of located objects tends to be uninterrupted (Vandeloise 2007: 43).

From the above classification of containers, two important findings can be obtained.

Firstly, both geometrical and functional attributes play an important part in defining an object as a container. On the one hand, geometrical attributes seem to bear more relevance to the prototypicality of containers. Of the four topological parameters mentioned above, dimensionality contributes most to defining a container, next is hollowness, closeness and discreteness come last. As there is more deviation from the prototype in terms of geometrical attributes, the members move along the continuum of prototypicality from the most prototypical instance to the most peripheral one. On the other hand, the sharing in the function of location control motivates the cognitive operations on certain kinds of deviating attributes in such a way that the objects varying widely in topological shapes are subsumed under the CONTAINER category.

Secondly, the family resemblance between members exhibit two characteristics. To start with, the attributes that contribute to putting the objects differing in size or shape into one category are not necessarily category-wide (Ungerer & Schmid 2001: 26). The family resemblance between members is established in various aspects. Some converge in dimensionality, some in closure, and others in discreteness. The next important feature is that the different members seem to be connected through chains (Taylor 2001: 108). As shown in the above analysis, between the most prototypical containers and the least prototypical ones, there is no feature that is shared by them at all. They are just indirectly connected through the medium of the intermediate members.

To recapitulate, the above analysis demonstrates that the instances of the CONTAINER category that correspond with the schematic landmark profiled by the preposition *in* vary widely in dimensionality, hollowness, closeness and discreteness. The most prototypical containers are the objects that are three-dimensional, hollow, fully enclosed and discrete, whereas the least prototypical containers are the one-dimensional objects. What follows is a comparison of the CONTAINER category between English and Chinese.

4.3 A Cross-linguistic Comparison of the CONTAINER Category

The previous contrastive studies on the similarities and dissimilarities in spatial categorization between English and Chinese mostly focus on the semantic or conceptual categories of spatial prepositions and their Chinese equivalents (Ma 2007; Zhang & Liu 2013). Few studies show much concern about the conceptual categories of the nominal predicates collocating with prepositions. And besides, a dualistic approach is usually taken to the analysis of cross-linguistic sameness and difference. Actually, the language distance exhibits a continuum of equivalence with full equivalence and zero equivalence at the two ends. Between the two ends is a range of partial equivalence, which has been empirically verified as a big trouble to L2 learners (Bohnacker & Rosen 2008; Jarvis & Pavlenko 2008; Tokowicz & MacWhinney 2005; Trofimovich, et al. 2007). Thus, the following corpus-based comparative study is focused on the conceptual categories of the nouns denoting reference objects, in which the cross-linguistic equivalence in categorizing containers will be revealed and depicted along a continuum.

4.3.1 A Corpus-based Approach to the Comparative Study

One advantage of corpus-based studies is that the exploration of language use and its cognitive underpinnings is not based on introspective data but data occurring naturally in real linguistic context (Xiao 2009). Therefore, a corpus linguistics-based approach is taken in the research. In comparative studies, parallel corpora are preferred because they can "increase our knowledge of language specific, typological and cultural differences and universal features" (Aijmer & Altenberg 1996: 12) by presenting "how the same content is expressed in two languages" (Aijmer & Altenberg 1996: 13). However, a problem with parallel corpora is the translationese (Gellerstam 1996; Qin & Wang 2004; Granger 2010) in the translated texts under the influence of the source language. For instance,

(72) They told him how he used to be very old, used to be wheeled about <u>in a garden-chair</u>.

他们告诉他说爷爷很老,从前老是坐<u>在轮椅里面</u>给推来推去。(GCEPC)

The expression *lun yi li mian* is seldom used by Chinese speakers. In the light of CCLC, *lun yi* is more likely to be categorized as a supporting surface and conventionally combines with *shang*.

To address this deficiency, two comparable corpora are employed as reference corpora in the comparative studies. Compared with parallel corpora, comparable corpora are more advantageous in providing spontaneous native data without the interference of other languages (Granger 2010). Considering this, both the parallel corpus and the comparable corpus are used to collect three types of data: English-Chinese bilingual data from General Chinese-English Parallel Corpus (GCEPC), English monolingual data from British National Corpus (BNC), and Chinese monolingual data from Peking University-Center for Chinese Linguistics-Corpus (CCLC). A qualitative analysis of the data is conducted in the following four steps: (1) Searching the sentence containing the expressions *in* + (*determiner*) + *N* and its corresponding Chinese translations from GCEPC; (2) Excluding metaphorical uses of *in*; (3) Identifying whether the spatial expression used in the Chinese translation is the translation equivalent of *in*; (4) Searching similar English and Chinese expressions from BNC and CCLC to confirm the similarity or difference observed in Step 2; (5) Following Jarvis' (2007) definition of concept and Pavlenko's (2009) classification of cross-linguistic conceptual equivalence, the data were coded and categorized. It is illustrated by Examples (73)-(75):

(73) He was in the public dock. [EVI Difference in Prototype]
他站在被告席上。(GCEPC)

(74) Mr. Gore stood in the dock looking straight ahead as the charges were read to him. [EVI Difference in Prototype] (BNC)

(75) 杨国富站在被告席上。[EVI Difference in Prototype] (CCLC)
Yang Guofu zhan zai beigao xi shang.
Yang Guofu stood at defendant table on
'Yang Guofu stood in the dock'.

EVI stands for the sixth type of equivalence in which English and Chinese differ in the construal of the prototype of a category. Firstly, *in the public dock* and its corresponding Chinese translation are searched from the parallel corpus. Secondly, a spatial expression that is not conceptually equivalent to *in* is observed in Chinese translation and marked in red. Thirdly, the frequency of the expression *in the public dock* is searched in BNC to make sure *in* is conventionally combined with *public dock* in English. Fourthly, the frequency of *bei gao xi shang* is searched in CCLC to make sure *shang* is conventionally combined with *bei gao xi* in Chinese. Fifthly, in the light of Jarvis' definition of concept, Pavlenko's classification of equivalence and prototype theory, the difference is categorized.

4.3.2 Degrees of Cross-linguistic Equivalence in the CONTAINER Category

Based on the analysis of the above three sources of data, a continuum of degrees of cross-linguistic equivalence in the CONTAINER category between English and Chinese is established.

The first degree of equivalence (Equivalence I) refers to the equivalence that object concepts profiled by English nouns and their Chinese equivalents are both construed as instances of the CONTAINER category. Related to the types of containers classified as above, Type I and Type VII containers have the maximum possibility of arriving at such a full equivalence in categorization. For example,

(76) I flew to Miss Mills, whom I saw by stealth in a back kitchen where there was a mangle.
跑到米尔斯小姐家去,在后面一间厨房里放烫衣机的地方偷偷地见到米尔斯小姐。(GCEPC)

(77) He would rather walk a mile in the rain to see for her carriage in the line at Gaunt House.
在屋子前面排列着的马车里面把她的车子找来,要他在雨里跑上整整一里路也愿意。(GCEPC)

The full equivalence in Type I containers is mostly motivated by the common neural architecture of the human brain and similar bodily experience of containment. For Type VII containers which are the most marginal members of the category, the motivation for the equivalence mainly derives from similar perceptual experience. As shown in Example (76), the line is perceived as a delimited area in which each carriage stands. If the carriage moves out, it will not be included in the line of carriages.

In the case of the second degree of Equivalence (Equivalence II), English and Chinese are nearly fully equivalent in that while the Chinese equivalents of English nouns are construed in more than one way in accordance with the perspectives taken by the viewers, CONTAINER is a more acceptable pattern of categorization. See the following examples,

(78) Your life is in your own hands.
你的生命攥在你自己手里。(GCEPC)

(79) Keeping the pencil in your hand. (BNC)

(80) Place a matchbox on your hand. (BNC)

(81) 一颗心撕成两半，一半攥在你手里。

yi ke xin si cheng liang ban, yi ban zuan zai ni shou li.

One-CL heart tear into two half one half hold at you hand in

'A heart is torn into two halves and one half is held in your hand'. (CCLC)

(82) 这一辈子攥在你手上了。

zhe yi beizi zuan zai ni shou shang le.

This one-CL life hold at you hand on le-ACTL

'The whole life is held in your hand'. (CCLC)

As shown in CCLC, the two expressions *zai ni shou li* and *zai ni shou shang* occur 159 times and 40 times respectively. This indicates that the conceptual referent of *hand* falls into two distinct categories in Chinese: CONTAINER and SUPPORTING SURFACE, but CONTAINER is more acceptable in Chinese. Compared with the language distance in Equivalence I, the language distance in Equivalence II is a little longer, but convergence between English and Chinese is still more prominent. Therefore, it is named as "near equivalence" which is a term borrowed from Pavlenko (2009: 133). The equivalence in categorizing the hand as a container might be attributed to the similar perceptual and functional experience with the hand. When an object is held by a hand, the fingers will be bent to form a hollow region within which the object is tightly located.

Evidence can also be found in construing less prototypical containers. For example,

(83) Romantic love is like an oasis in the desert. (BNC)

(84) 这就是沙漠里的绿洲。

zhe jiushi shamo li de lvzhou.

this is desert in De_1 oasis

'This is the oasis in the desert'. (CCLC)

(85) 沙漠上的绿洲对于骆驼队一样的新鲜可爱。

shangmo shang de lvzhou duiyu luotuo dui yiyang de xinxian keai.

desert on De_1 oasis for camel team same De fresh pretty

'For the caravan, the oasis in the desert is equally fresh and pretty'. (CCLC)

As shown in CCLC, there are 80 instances of *sha mo li* and 30 instances of *sha mo shang*. This indicates that the conceptual referent of *desert* also splits into two distinct categories in Chinese: CONTAINER and SUPPORTING SURFACE, but CONTAINER is more prototypical in Chinese. According to the above classification of prototypicality, the desert is described as an atypical container by being two-dimensional and vaguely bounded. Despite the non-prototypicality, both languages tend to arrive at an agreement in categorization of the desert. This demonstrates prototypicality is not a necessary condition for the realization of cross-linguistic equivalence in categorization.

However, as regards the third degree of equivalence (Equivalence III), the divergence between English and Chinese increases with Chinese, in contrast with English, showing less preference for the CONTAINER category. This is illustrated in Examples (86)-(90).

(86) In the sad moonlight, she clasped him by the neck and lad her face upon his chest.
她在凄清的月光下搂住了爸爸的脖子，把脸靠在他的胸脯上。(GECPC)

(87) In the moonlight I walked sadly around. (BNC)

(88) As he walked beneath the moonlight, was he thinking of Nina? (BNC)

(89) 傍晚，他们一起在月光下散步。
bang wan tamen yiqi zai yue guang xia sanbu.
near evening they together at moon light under walk
'At dusk, they walked in the moonlight together'. (CCLC)

(90) 他在月光中走得很轻。
ta zai yue guang zhong zou de hen qing.
he at moon light in walk De_2 very light
'He walked in the moonlight with light steps'. (CCLC)

As shown in CCLC, *yue guang zhong/li* and *yue guang xia* have a frequency ratio of 153 : 741, whereas retrieval of *in the moonlight* and *beneath the moonlight* in BNC shows that the frequency ratio is 139 : 3. This suggests that in Chinese, light is more likely to be categorized as a covering that is situated high above the located object. The diversity in categorization implies that the two nouns, *light* and *yue guang* actually do not fully overlap in the profiled conceptual referent. In the conceptual structure of *yue guang*, the conceptual feature [shielding] is given more prominence than the feature [containing]. As a result, the schematic landmark profiled by the locative marker *xia* is more likely to be elaborated.

Categorization is not merely made horizontally with members being extended from the prototype through family resemblance, but also hierarchically around a basic-level category (Lakoff 1987: 30). The fourth degree of equivalence (Equivalence IV) just refers to the cross-linguistic difference in the hierarchical categorization. Within this type of equivalence, object concepts profiled by the Chinese nouns sometimes are subsumed within a category subordinate to the CONTAINER category. For example,

(91) I could see Mac watching me in his rearview mirror.
我能看见迈克正从后视镜里望着我。(GCEPC)

(92) Joseph studied the face of the driver in the rearview mirror. (BNC)
我从后视镜里看到他的脸。
wo cong houshi jing li kandao ta de lian.
I from rearview mirror in see he De_1 face
'I saw his face in the rearview mirror'. (CCLC)

In the above examples, the object concepts profiled by *rearview mirror* and its Chinese equivalent *hou shi jing* are on the one hand all included in the superordinate category REFERENCE OBJECT, but on the other hand, they are in two categories of different levels of generality. To be more specific, the *rearview mirror* is construed as an instance of CONTAINER, whereas *hou shi jing* is further specified as a type of container that serves as a path of motion which is subordinate to the former, as demonstrated in Figure 4.1.

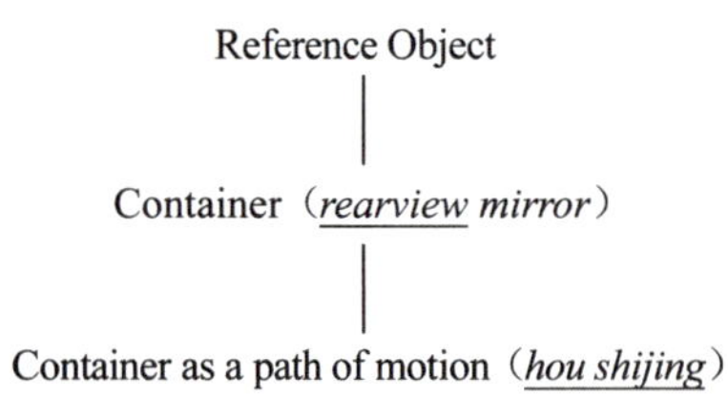

Figure 4.1 Levels of Categorization

A point to mention is that with the variation in the hierarchical level of category, a factual perception event designated by *in the rearview mirror* is construed as a fictive motion event (Talmy 2000: 115-116) in Chinese, which is encoded by the expression *cong* + *N*. In English, a fictive motion event is usually expressed by *from/through* + *N*. Therefore, the Chinese expression *cong*+*N*+*li* falls into two linguistic categories in English: *in*+*N* and *from/through*+*N*, but *cong*+*N*+*li* and *from/through*+*N* are much closer in form and conceptual representations.

It can be seen that in the case of Type III and Type IV equivalence, there are both overlaps and disparities between English and Chinese in the pattern of categorization. This is referred to as partial equivalence (Pavlenko 2009: 134). In comparison with the above two types of equivalence, there is an increasing typological distance between English and Chinese in the CONTAINER category.

As to the sixth degree of equivalence (Equivalence VI), object concepts profiled by the Chinese nouns are not construed as instances of CONTAINER with a different perspective favored by Chinese. This is termed "zero equivalence" in the categorization between English and Chinese. As is mentioned above, one cannot verbalize experience without taking a perspective favored by the language being used (Slobin 1996: 107). Under the influence of language-specific perspective, certain aspects of a reference object are selectively highlighted to represent the whole. This is what Talmy termed schematization (2000: 177) which largely accounts for the cross-linguistic difference in categorization. For example,

(93) A catbird, the Northern mocker, lit in a tree over Tom's head.
有一只猫鹊——一种北方的学舌鸟——在汤姆头顶上的一棵大树上落下来。(GCEPC)

(94) Last spring, there had been a blackbird's nest in the tree. (BNC)
街道两旁树上鸟窝很多。
jiedao liang pang shu shang niao wo hen duo.
street two side tree on bird nest very many
'There are many nests in the trees on both sides of the road'. (CCLC)

Obviously, the tree existing in the objective world remains unchanged and what is changed is the parts of the tree that enter the mental eyes of speakers. Directed by the English-specific schematization, the speaker zooms in on the crown bounded by branches within which the bird or the bird's nest is located or hidden, whereas Chinese native speakers' attention is drawn to the branch on which the bird or the bird's nest stands. Evidence for such zero equivalence is more frequently found in construal of Type II and Type III containers.

(95) He had sat in his saddle some half-hour, taking note of these things.
他在马背上观察着这一切，等了大约半个小时之后。(GCEPC)

(96) They are often expected to spend days on the march, even sleeping in the saddle. (BNC)

(97) 他却在马鞍上打瞌睡。
ta que zai ma'an shang da keshui.
he but at saddle on beat doze
'But he dozed off in the saddle'. (CCLC)

The partially enclosed saddle is construed as an instance of CONTAINER by manipulating the mental completion of the material boundary with a horizontal plane, however, in Chinese the attention is drawn to the bottom of the saddle to the neglect of the concavity of the saddle. More evidence could be found in construal of Type III containers.

(98) I don't want Frederick to trample a hole in my muslin frock.
我可不愿意弗莱特立克在我细纱袍子上踩个洞。(GCEPC)

In the same vein, the family resemblance between the solid object frock and the prototypical container is established by means of functionally motivated conceptual projection from the domain of hollowness to that of solidness. This also does not take place in Chinese which is more liable to conceptualize the hole as an object fixed on the surface of the frock rather than a part embedded in the frock. All in all, language-specific perspectives serve as filters through which the aspects that are most relevant to the immediate demands of the speakers are preserved to be verbalized.

The seventh degree of equivalence (Equivalence VII) is another type of zero equivalence in which the object concepts profiled by the Chinese nouns are not construed as instances of CONTAINER with cross-linguistic disparities in prototypical examples of the categories denoted by the nouns. A series of experiments and discussions on the cross-linguistic difference in the internal category structures have indicated that prototypes are not universal but are culture-dependent (Ungerer & Schmid 2001: 50-52). As Cruse (1990: 389) argued, the prototype of a given category is formed against the cultural background where a person grows up. For example, persons living in Antarctic will have a different prototype of the BIRD category from persons living in Amazon Basin or Sahara Desert. Similarly, people growing up and living in

China will have a different mental representation of the best example of the PULPIT category from the English native speakers:

(99) However stern he might show himself in the pulpit.
无论他在布道台上显得多么声色俱厉.(GCEPC)

(100) Richard Baxter stayed in the pulpit. (BNC)

(101) 结婚预告在牧师的讲道台上宣布出来了。
jiehun yugao zai mushi de jiangdao tai shang xuanbu
marriage banns at priest De_1 preach platform on announce
chu lai le.
out come le-ARTC
'The banns were put up in the pulpit'. (CCLC)

The comparison of the explanations of *pulpit* and *budaotai* provided by *Oxford English Dictionary* and *Contemporary Chinese Dictionary* reveals that [enclosing] is an important conceptual feature contained in the concept of the word *pulpit*, but the Chinese expression *budaotai* highlights the feature [a surface for a priest to stand on] with the use of *tai* which refers to a flat platform high above the ground. This suggests that English and Chinese differ in the prototype of the PULPIT category. The English-based prototype is a three-dimensional container in which the priest gives his sermons, whereas the Chinese-based one is a platform on which the priest stands.

To sum up, there are seven types of cross-linguistic equivalence in the CONTAINER category between English and Chinese. Similar to the prototypicality of containers, the cross linguistic equivalence in categorization is also not binary in nature, but exhibits a continuum of equivalence ranging from full equivalence, partial equivalence to zero equivalence. But the two continua do not correspond with each other; to be more specific, strong prototypicality does not necessarily presuppose a high degree of equivalence. As is noted above, English and Chinese arrive at a full equivalence in categorizing the marginal containers by sharing similar functional experience. Conversely, in the case of Type II and Type III containers which are much more prototypical than Type VII, the two languages differ most. Such a lack of correspondence complicates the cognitive process of the use of English spatial preposition *in* by Chinese-speaking learners of English. Therefore, a deeper exploration of how categorization affects learners'use of *in* is needed.

As hypothesized in Chapter Three, as far as bilingual learners are concerned, the elaborative distance between the object concept profiled by the noun and the schematic landmark profiled by the preposition *in* will be put under the influence of both prototypicality and degrees of cross-linguistic equivalence. From a developmental perspective, at the early stage of English learning, the use of *in* by Chinese-speaking learners is conceptually motivated by degrees of cross-linguistic equivalence which are more important in defining the elaborative distance and constitutes the conceptual mechanism of L1 transfer. But as exposure to L2 input increases, the effect of prototypicality will be strengthened, and thus cause a gradual decrease in conceptual transfer from L1.

To test the above hypothesis, the researcher, based on the above two classificatory frameworks, intends to make an empirical study of the effects of prototypicality and degrees of equivalence in the CONTAINER category on the use of *in* by Chinese-speaking English learners at different levels of L2 proficiency.

4.4 Summary

This chapter, by taking a prototype approach, makes a detailed analysis of how a reference object is construed as a container within and across speech communities in which a continuum of prototypicality and a continuum of degrees of cross-linguistic equivalence are established respectively. On the basis of the two continua, the empirical investigation of the occurrence of conceptual transfer and its developmental change will be conducted.

Chapter Five Research Methodology

5.1 Introduction

This chapter starts with presentation of research questions in Section 5. 2. The introduction of research design is made in Section 5. 3 and is followed by the operational definition of L2 proficiency in Section 5. 4. Participants recruited in the study are described in Section 5. 5. This chapter concludes with the discussion of data collection, procedure and data analysis.

5.2 Research Questions

To test the hypothesized effects of prototypicality and the degree of cross-linguistic equivalence on the use of *in* by L2 learners, the study attempts to address the following four questions:

1. How does prototypicality of members of the CONTAINER category affect learners' use of the English spatial preposition *in*?

2. How does prototypicality effect change with the increase of L2 proficiency?

3. How do degrees of cross-linguistic equivalence in the CONTAINER category affect learners' use of the English spatial preposition *in*?

4. How does the effect of degrees of cross-linguistic equivalence change with the increase of L2 proficiency?

5.3 Research Design

Inasmuch as the purpose of the research is to investigate how conceptual transfer occurs and changes over time in the process of L2 acquisition, an ideal approach to the issue should be a longitudinal one which can track a number of sampled individuals over an extended period of time. Regrettably, a cross-sectional approach, known as "pseudo-longitudinal approach" (Jarvis & Pavlenko 2008: 37) is used as a replacement. To track the occurrence of conceptual transfer in relation to developmental changes in L2 proficiency, data are collected from three different proficiency groups. The assumption underlying the cross-section design is that "comparing [multiple] groups would yield results similar to what would be found if we looked at a single individual over time" (Gass & Selinker 2001: 33).

In this empirical study, prototypicality and degrees of cross-linguistic equivalence are two within-group variables, and L2 proficiency is a between-group variable. In accordance with Chapter Four, the effect of prototypicality is measured at seven levels and the effect of degrees of equivalence is measured at six levels.

Two types of data are collected: data on learners' use of *in* in different prototypical and typological contexts and data on the verification of L1 transfer in learners' use of *in*. The instrument used to elicit learner data is a preposition test consisting of 65 multiple-choice questions. The test questions are partly taken from previous studies (Ma 2005; Wei 2007; Li & Cai 2008) and are partly designed by the researcher specifically for the study. As to evidence for L1 transfer, four types of comparisons are made and a retrospective interview is conducted to confirm the effect of L1 transfer in learners' use of *in*.

5.4 Operational Definition of L2 Proficiency

In empirical research on L2 acquisition, variables often present themselves as abstract or fuzzy concepts which are difficult to measure or observe directly.

Therefore, provision of operational definitions of variables concerned before a study is carried out is considered essential (Wen 2004: 34). Through operationalization, the abstract concepts are transformed into what can be quantified. In this study, an important variable needing to be operationalized is L2 proficiency. Theoretically, L2 proficiency can be defined as a person's overall competence and ability to perform in L2 (Thomas 1994: 330). For the sake of measurement, it is usually transformed into two factors: Scores in proficiency tests and the length of exposure to L2. A review of conceptual transfer research shows that length of L2 exposure is preferred (Jarvis & Odlin 2000; Malt & Sloman 2003; Daller, et al. 2011; Zhang & Liu 2013) as an index of participants' L2 proficiency because the purpose of conceptual transfer research is to investigate whether and how learners' L1-based conceptualization of the world is restructured with the accumulation of L2 learning experience. Considering Chinese learners of English living in an L1 dominant environment are mostly exposed to L2 input in the classroom, the present study operationalizes L2 proficiency as the number of years of formal L2 instruction that the participants had received (Jarvis & Pavlenko 2008: 199).

5.5 Participants

Class-based convenience sampling is used in the study for the easy availability of participants. 150 Chinese learners of English from Shandong Province are recruited in the research. According to the length of formal instruction, they are divided into three proficiency groups with 50 participants in each: low, intermediate and high (Table 5.1). The low proficiency group consists of Senior Two students aged 15-17 from a senior middle school, who have had four years of formal classroom English learning and are preparing for the national college entrance examinations. The intermediate group consists of first-year English majors aged 17-19 from a normal university in Shandong Province, who have been learning English for six years and are working hard for the Test for English Majors Band 4. The high group consists of third-year English majors aged 19-21 from the same university who have had 8-year formal English education and are preparing for the Test for English Majors

Band 8. In addition, three participants from each proficiency group are selected to attend the follow-up interview. For the sake of convenience, the low, intermediate and high proficiency groups will be hereafter abbreviated as LG, IG and HG respectively.

Table 5. 1 ***Background of Participants***

	Level	Years of Learning	Age	Number
1	Low	4	15-17	50
2	Intermediate	6	17-19	50
3	High	8	19-21	50

5.6 Instruments

As mentioned in the above, two types of data are collected: Learners' use of the spatial preposition *in* and evidence for the occurrence of L1 transfer. The former is elicited via a preposition test and the latter is obtained by a series of comparisons and a retrospective interview.

5.6.1 Preposition Test

The instrument used to elicit learners' use of *in* is a preposition test consisting of 65 multiple-choice questions. The reasons why a multiple-choice instead of a free gap-fill is used are as follows: (1) With the provision of potential answers, it will reduce the cognitive load of participants, senior school students in particular who are always required to do multiple-choice exercises in class; (2) It will to some extent prevent the participants from producing answers that defy explanations and will be more advantageous to elicit information serving the research purpose well (Alderson, Clapham & Wall 2000: 45).

Four attempts are made to improve the validity of the test. Firstly, to reduce the probability of guessing and eliminating implausible distracters, the prepositions which partially overlap in conceptual representations are provided as distracters in the test, like *on*, *under*, *through*, *over* and etc. Of the 65 multiple questions, 27 are designed to elicit the use of these distracters and are randomly arranged into the test paper.

Secondly, great care is taken in the question design which is highly related to the content validity of the test. Following the two classificatory frameworks established in Chapter Four, the nouns that refer to the reference objects of different prototypicality and represent different degrees of cross-linguistic equivalence are selected and categorized. The sentences containing the nouns are partly borrowed from the previous studies (Ma 2005; Wei 2007; Li & Cai 2008) and partly selected from BNC with some necessary adaptations, like simplifying the sentence structures to make them easier to be understood by senior school students. Two colleagues are invited to work with the researcher to check whether all prototypicality and degrees of equivalence have been covered and to identify what each item is intended to test. Additionally, two American high school teachers are paid to help proofread the paper to guarantee the authenticity and naturalness of the sentences.

Thirdly, in the light of the studies by Correa-Beningfield (1985) and by Ma (2005), in this study there are at least four items in a set that consistently test the same prototypicality or degrees of equivalence. The mean score of each set is used as the index of the effect of each level of prototypicality or equivalence on learners' use of *in*. The set testing Equivalence VI includes two items that elicit the use of the preposition *on* because there is difficulty in finding enough appropriate instances related to the use of *in*.

The following is an example of a set of items designed for Type I containers.

(102) a. There is a cage ________ the bird.

b. The boy ________ the telephone box.

c. Is there any wine ________ the bottle?

d. Listen to the noises ________ the classroom.

e. There are some candies ________ the jar.

In this set, the nouns behind the blanks all refer to the containers that are three dimensional, closed, hollow and discrete.

Fourthly, below each test item there is a corresponding picture to illustrate the spatial scene described by the sentence. This is proposed as a method to provide more contextual information to reduce the potential ambiguity and simultaneously to facilitate the mapping between words and their real world referents (Pavlenko 2009: 131). Actually, the picture-elicited production of target language has been widely practiced in the research related to the acquisition of spatial coding systems (Bowerman & Choi 2003; Jarvis & Odlin 2000; Ma 2005; Wei 2007; Li & Cai 2008). As to the sentences that are borrowed from previous studies (Ma 2005; Wei 2007; Li & Cai 2008), the corresponding pictures are also borrowed from them, and as to the sentences designed by the researcher, the pictures are downloaded from the image search engine Google (http://image.google.com).

The directions of the test are written in Chinese and an example is given to demonstrate the spatial concept represented by the spatial preposition and to instruct participants how to perform the task. For the possible new words, the Chinese translations are provided in the brackets and simultaneously the teachers of the participants are asked to integrate the words naturally in their teaching resources before administering the test.

5.6.2 Tasks to Collect Evidence of L1 Transfer

In this research, four types of comparisons are made (Table 5.2) and a follow-up interview is conducted to collect evidence of cross-linguistic effects.

Since the factors influencing the process of L2 acquisition are miscellaneous, the misuse of a preposition is not necessarily attributable to L1 transfer. This calls for multiple sources of evidence to disentangle L1 influence from other factors. Following Jarvis' (2010) refined methodological framework for investigating L1 transfer, four types of comparisons are made to collect four types of evidence. The first one is a comparison of learner data for each prototypical context or each degree of cross-linguistic equivalence whereby transfer will be confirmed on the basis of commonness in the use of prepositions among the participants. Such evidence is called "intragroup homogeneitys" (Jarvis 2010: 172). Take the following item as an example.

(103) There is a car ________ the square.

If the misuse of the preposition *on* is shared by the majority of participants, a tentative conclusion about the occurrence of L1 negative transfer can be made.

The second comparison of learner data is made across different degrees of equivalence to collect evidence of intralingual contrast (Jarvis 2010: 172), which means that the diversity in learner data across the typological contexts might be attributable to their different degrees of equivalence with L1. For example,

(104) a. There is a bird ________ the cage.

b. There is a car ________ the square.

According to the classification of degrees of cross-linguistic equivalence in the CONTAINER category, there is greater equivalence in categorizing the cage than the square. If there are more misuses of *on* observed in Example (104)b than in (104)a, the effects of negative transfer and positive transfer will both be supported.

The third comparison is made between learner data and the corresponding L1 data to seek evidence of cross-language congruity (Jarvis 2010: 173), which refers to the correspondence between the two types of data. In other words, if learners' choice of English prepositions parallels their L1 lexical choice while performing the same task, occurrence of L1 transfer will be confirmed. This type of evidence is elicited through the task of immediate translation which is claimed to be an effective yet simple way to track the participants' L1-based conceptualization of the world (Cai 2009: 55). Specifically speaking, two sentences are selected from each set of items for testing the effect of degrees of equivalence and the participants are asked to translate them into Chinese as soon as they fill in the blanks with appropriate prepositions. Then, an identification of the correspondence between the spatial preposition chosen to complete the sentence and the L1 spatial expression is made. For instance, if the participants are observed to use *on* in "There is a car in the square" and to translate the sentence as "*guangchang shang you yiliang che*", there will be the evidence of L1 transfer.

The fourth is a comparison between learner data and English native data which are mainly gained from BNC. If there is cross-linguistic difference in the preferential choice of prepositions which correspond with the conceptual differences identified in Section 4.3, effects of L1-specific concepts on the use of *in* will be confirmed.

Table 5.2 ***Types of Comparisons for Collecting Evidence of L1 Transfer***
(Adapted from Jarvis 2010)

Types of comparison	Types of evidence	Significance
Comparison of learner data in a given context	intragroup homogeneity	Transfer will be confirmed if the choice of the preposition is shared by the learners of the same L1.
Comparison between learner data across the degrees of equivalence	intralingual contrast	Transfer will be confirmed if the conceptual categories are found to be different in transferrability with their different degrees of similarity with L1.
Comparison between learner data and corresponding L1 data	cross-language congruity	Transfer will be confirmed if there is correspondence between the use of the English preposition and the use of the Chinese spatial expression.
Comparison between learner data and English native data	cross-language disparity	Transfer will be confirmed if there is disparity in choice of the preposition between learner data and native data.

Apart from the above comparisons, a follow-up interview is also conducted to elicit participants' retrospective reports about their thought processes while taking the preposition test. In comparison with other data-collection methods, interview is more advantageous in obtaining information about feelings, thoughts and intentions (Wen 2004: 158). Three steps are taken in the retrospective interview. First of all, immediately after the completion of the test, the teacher in charge of each proficiency group scores the performance of the participants and ranks their performance as excellent, good and failure respectively. Secondly, in each proficiency group, three participants, each of whom represents one grade (excellent, good and failure), are randomly selected. And finally, the teacher presents them with their own test papers and prompts them to recall and answer the following questions: Is this item easy or difficult? When you dealt with this item, which language firstly occurred in your mind, Chinese or English? Do you think it is quite similar to L1 or different from L1? Why did you choose the preposition? All the questions are presented and answered in Chinese.

The combination of the above five types of evidence renders it possible to get data cross-checked against each other to confirm that L1-related effects are at play or not at play in learners' choice of a preposition. And more importantly, it is also contributory to providing a fuller characterization of the nature, strength, pervasiveness, and independence or interdependence of L1 influence relative to other factors (Jarvis 2010: 54).

5.7 Procedure

The research procedure consists of three steps. Firstly, a pilot study is administered to check the validity of the preposition test. 10 participants are selected from the parallel classes in the same grade as the participants of the real test. On average it takes them 35 minutes to finish the test. And the follow-up interview with the participants reveals that the words and the sentence structures are not beyond them and the pictures arouse their interest in the task to some extent.

Secondly, the formal preposition test is taken in class under the supervision of their teachers. Before the test starts, a short chat about prepositions is made between the teachers and the participants as a warm-up. And then the participants are encouraged to choose prepositions based on their intuitions of the spatial relations as depicted in the pictures. While taking the test, power point slides are presented for fear that the pictures printed on the paper are not clear to the participants. The participants are required to finish it independently without consulting dictionaries and other reference books.

The final step is to elicit learners' self-reports through retrospective interview. Immediately after the test, the teachers evaluate and classify the participants' performance as excellent, good and failure with the help of their colleagues, and then three participants from each proficiency group are selected for the interview. As required by the researcher, the teacher starts the interview with a brief chat with the participants about the test, which goes like "What do you think of the test?" or "Have you ever encountered such a test format?" for the sake of establishing a harmonious relationship with each other. Following this chat, the teacher focuses the subjects on the items related to the use of preposition *in* and asks them to recall the thought processes underlying their use of prepositions with the guidance of a series of pre-designed questions.

Throughout the test and the retrospective interview, the verbal exchanges between the teachers and participants are performed in Chinese. At the end of the experiment, all the teachers and participants involved in the study are given a gift in return for their great help and active cooperation.

5.8 Data Analysis

Data analysis in the study mainly includes scoring of the preposition test and statistical analysis of the quantitative data.

Scoring of the test is mainly intended to find out how frequent the prepositions under investigation are used in each prototypical or typological context. Therefore, the 27 distracting items are excluded from scoring. In comparison with BNC, for each choice corresponding with the preferred use of English native speakers, one point is awarded. Since the number of items is not the same across the sets, the score of each set is the ratio between the appropriate uses of the prepositions and the number of items within this set. Take the set of items for Type I containers in Section 5. 6. 1 as an example. Altogether five items are included in this set. Each participant's use of *in* in each item is summed up and divided by five, then, the final number is the score he gains in this prototypical context. The scores are entered into the computer for statistical analysis by SPSS (Statistical Package of Social Science).

The statistical analysis of the quantitative data is made to address the following four issues: (1) The significant difference in the use of *in* across different prototypical contexts; (2) The significant difference in the use of *in* for a specific prototypical context across three proficiency groups; (3) The significant difference in the use of *in* across different degrees of equivalence; (4) The significant difference in the use of *in* for a specific degree of equivalence across three proficiency groups. To this end, repeated measures ANOVA is run with prototypicality or degrees of equivalence as a within-group variable and L2 proficiency as a between-group variable. All the quantitative data are treated by SPSS 13.0. The statistical significance level is set at the default value of 0.05.

5.9 Summary

Following the discussions on what problem the study intends to solve in the above chapters, this chapter deals with how the problem is solved with a detailed account of the methodological approach taken by the study. As mentioned in the foregoing discussion, 150 Chinese learners of English at three developmental stages participate in the study. Guided by research questions, two types of data are collected: Learners' use of *in* and evidence of L1 transfer. The instrument used to collect the first type of data is a preposition test consisting of 65 multiple questions. And the tasks for eliciting the second type of data include four types of comparisons and a retrospective interview. Finally the chapter describes the scoring of the paper and the statistical analysis of the quantitative data. In the next chapter, a detailed delineation of the results of the study is offered and in its wake the discussions on the results related to the above research questions will be done.

Chapter Six Results and Discussion

6.1 Introduction

This chapter focuses on reporting and interpreting the results of the study. Section 6.2 presents the results of the participants' use of the English spatial preposition *in* in different prototypical contexts and results of the use of *in* in a particular context for each proficiency group. Then in Section 6.3 the participants' use of *in* in different typological contexts and the use of *in* in a particular typological context for each proficiency group are reported. This chapter concludes with the discussion of the results in respect to the research questions.

6.2 Results of the Effect of Prototypicality

As illustrated in Chapter Four, the containers that correspond with the landmark profiled by *in* are classified into seven groups in terms of prototypicality. The discussion on the formation of the composite structure [IN + N] reveals that prototypicality is important in defining the elaborative distance between the schematic container profiled by *in* and the instances evoked by the nominal predicates. Therefore, the use of *in* for English natives tends to increase with advancing prototypicality. Then does the use of *in* for L2 learners also increase as degrees of prototypicality rise? Does the effect of prototypicality change with the increase in L2 experience? The results reported in Section 6. 2. 1 and Section 6. 2. 2 will provide answers to the two questions.

6.2.1 Use of *in* across Different Prototypical Contexts

This section is concerned with the results of the use of *in* across the seven prototypical contexts. Table 6. 1 presents descriptive statistics for the use of *in* in the seven prototypical contexts, mainly including the means and standard deviations. Table 6. 2 reports ANOVA test of the effect of prototypicality on the participants' responses. Table 6. 3 demonstrates results of pairwise comparisons which are performed to provide estimates of difference between each pair of prototypical contexts (Landu & Everitt 2004).

The descriptive statistics in Table 6. 1 show that the use of *in* is different across the seven prototypical contexts. The results of ANOVA tests in Table 6. 2 demonstrate that the difference across the contexts is significant, $F(6, 882)=114.263$, $p=0.000<0.05$. This supports the significant effect of prototypicality on participants' use of *in*.

Table 6. 1 ***Descriptive Statistics for the Effect of Prototypicality on the Use of in***

Context of prototypicality	Mean	Standard deviation	N
Prototypical Context I	0. 754	0. 175	150
Prototypical Context II	0. 431	0. 171	
Prototypical Context III	0. 432	0. 232	
Prototypical Context IV	0. 712	0. 214	
Prototypical Context V	0. 451	0. 222	
Prototypical Context VI	0. 752	0. 195	
Prototypical Context VII	0. 735	0. 186	

Table 6. 2 ***Results of ANOVA Test of the Effect of Prototypicality***

Source	SS	Df	Mean Square	F	Sig.
Prototype	23. 243	6	3. 868	114. 263	0. 000
Error	29. 903	882	0. 034		

Despite the confirmation of the effect, there is no linear increase in the participants' preference for *in* with the rise of prototypicality as shown in Table

6.1 and Figure 6.1. This is well illustrated in the following two aspects:

Firstly, the use of *in* moves up and down across the seven types of containers. To be precise, the mean starts with the highest point (0.754) in Prototypical Context I and drops off substantially in Context II (0.431), reaching the lowest point. Then it undergoes a slight rise in Context III (0.432). After rising dramatically in Context IV (0.712), the mean suffers a sharp fall in Context V (0.451) again, but makes a significant recovery in Context VI (0.752), and then ends with a slight fall in Context VII (0.735).

Secondly, in Contexts I, IV, VI and VII, *in* is much more preferred than in Contexts II, III and V. Results of pairwise comparisons (see Table 6.3) further demonstrate that across Contexts I, IV, VI and VII, the use of *in* between each two of them is not significantly different, but each of the four contexts has significant difference from Contexts II, III and V respectively. Likewise, across Contexts II, III and V, the use of *in* between each two of them is not at significant variance, but each of them differs significantly from Contexts I, IV, VI and VII respectively. In other words, the variation in prototypicality across Contexts I, IV, VI and VII and the variation in prototypicality across Contexts II, III and V fails to cause a significant change in participants' use of *in*.

To sum up, the statistical analysis indicates that while prototypicality has a significant effect on participants' use of *in*, the use of *in* does not increase with rising prototypicality.

Table 6.3 ***Pairwise Comparisons of the Use of in across Seven Prototypical Contexts***

Prototypical Context	I	II	III	IV	V	VI	VII
I		0.323*	0.322*	0.042	0.303*	0.002	0.019
II	−0.323*		−0.001	−0.281*	−0.020	−0.321*	−0.304*
III	−0.322*	0.001		−0.280*	−0.019	−0.320*	−0.303*
IV	−0.042	0.281*	0.280*		0.261*	−0.040	−0.023
V	−0.303*	0.022	0.021	−0.261*		−0.301*	−0.284*
VI	−0.002	0.330*	0.329*	0.040	0.301*		0.017
VII	−0.019	0.303*	0.302*	0.023	0.284*	−0.017	

6.2.2 Use of *in* across Different Proficiency Groups

The effects of L2 proficiency on the use of *in* reported by the statistical analysis includes the main effect of L2 proficiency and the interaction effect of L2 proficiency and prototypicality. Table 6. 4 reports descriptive statistics for the use of *in* across three proficiency groups. Results of ANOVA test of the main effect and the interaction effect are showed by Table 6. 5. Table 6. 6 is concerned with the results of post hoc (Scheffe) test which is run to get more detailed information about which particular group differs significantly from each other. Finally Figure 6. 1 delineates the changes of responses caused by the interaction effect.

Descriptive statistics in Table 6. 4 show that in each prototypical context, participants' preference for *in* is different across the three proficiency groups. Except Contexts V and VI, the use of *in* for each prototypical context increases with advancing L2 proficiency. In Contexts V and VI, a U-shaped pattern of variation is exhibited across the groups by the mean of IG (Intermediate Group) being lower than that of LG (Low Group).

Table 6. 4 ***Descriptive Statistics for the Effect of Prototypicality across Three Proficiency Groups***

Prototypicality	Proficiency	Mean	Standard deviation	N
1	High	0. 853	0. 128	50
	Intermediate	0. 746	0. 158	50
	Low	0. 664	0. 184	50
2	High	0. 512	0. 148	50
	Intermediate	0. 398	0. 157	50
	Low	0. 389	0. 180	50
3	High	0. 467	0. 261	50
	Intermediate	0. 432	0. 237	50
	Low	0. 398	0. 191	50

Continued

Prototypicality	Proficiency	Mean	Standard deviation	N
4	High	0.844	0.168	50
	Intermediate	0.704	0.186	50
	Low	0.588	0.208	50
5	High	0.537	0.229	50
	Intermediate	0.403	0.211	50
	Low	0.414	0.214	50
6	High	0.825	0.141	50
	Intermediate	0.715	0.202	50
	Low	0.725	0.222	50
7	High	0.795	0.149	50
	Intermediate	0.735	0.223	50
	Low	0.675	0.162	50

The ANOVA test reported by Table 6.5 indicates that L2 proficiency has a significant main effect on the participants' use of *in* in seven prototypical contexts, $F(2, 882) = 34.133$, $p = 0.000 < 0.05$; in other words, the difference across the three proficiency groups mentioned above reaches the significant level.

Table 6.5 ***Results of ANOVA Test of the Effect of L2 Proficiency***

Source	SS	Df	Mean Square	F	Sig.
Proficiency	0.509	2	0.254	34.133	0.000
Prototype * Proficiency	0.783	12	0.065	1.924	0.028
Error	29.903	882	0.034		

The results of post hoc (Scheffe) test in Table 6.6 further demonstrate that the difference is significant between each pair of proficiency groups.

Table 6.6 ***Scheffe Test Results of the Difference in the Use of in between Groups***

Proficiency	High	Intermediate	Low
High		0.0985*	0.1386*
Intermediate	−0.0985*		0.0401*
Low	−0.1386*	−0.0401*	

* The mean difference is significant at the 0.05 level.

Apart from the main effect, the interaction effect between L2 proficiency and prototypicality is also significant as shown in Table 6.5, $F(12, 882) = 1.924$, $p = 0.028 < 0.05$. Put in plain words, the effect of prototypicality on the use of *in* is strengthened or weakened with the increase or decrease of L2 proficiency. It is well depicted in Figure 6.1, which reveals that the interaction effect is mainly evident in the following two aspects:

Firstly, in HG (High Group), the variation in participants' preference for *in* across the four contexts (Contexts I, IV, VI and VII), where *in* is used frequently, exhibits a linear decrease as prototypicality declines (0.853>0.844>0.825>0.795). In other words, the more prototypical the containers are, the more frequently *in* is used by HG. Across the two contexts (Contexts II and III) where the use of *in* remains at a low level, the number of *in* also decreases linearly from Context II to Context III (0.512>0.467).

Secondly, in LG, the number of *in* in Prototypical Context I is not the largest (0.664). To put it another way, LG does not use *in* most frequently in the most prototypical context.

In spite of the confirmation of the interaction effect, an important point to mention is that a linear change in the use of *in* across the seven prototypical contexts is not observed even in HG (Figure 6.1).

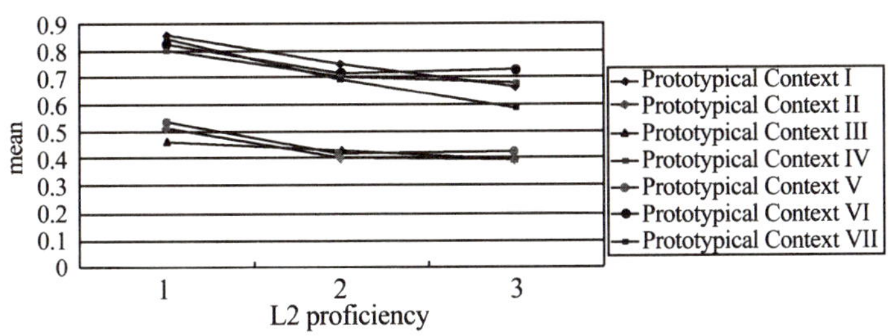

Figure 6.1 Interaction between L2 Proficiency and Prototypicality

To summarize, the statistical analysis indicates that L2 proficiency has a significant main effect on the participants' use of *in*. Except Contexts V and VI, the use of *in* increases with improving L2 proficiency. The interaction between L2 proficiency and prototypicality is also significant, but the linear rise in the use of *in* with the increase of prototypicality is only observed in HG.

6.3 Results of the Effect of Degrees of Equivalence

According to the model accounting for the formation of the construction [IN+N] by L2 learners, besides prototypicality, degrees of cross-linguistic equivalence in the CONTAINER category are also assumed to play an important role in defining the elaborative distance and constitute the conceptual mechanism of L1 transfer. In this section, the results about the effect of degrees of equivalence and its changes with L2 proficiency will be reported.

6.3.1 Use of *in* across Different Degrees of Cross-linguistic Equivalence

This section primarily deals with the results of the use of *in* across the six degrees of equivalence. Table 6.7 shows descriptive statistics for participants' responses across the six degrees of equivalence. Results of ANOVA test of the effect of degrees of equivalence on the participants' use of *in* are presented in Table 6.8. Table 6.9 reports the results of pairwise comparisons which are undertaken to further detect where the significant mean differences lie between the degrees of equivalence.

The descriptive statistics reported by Table 6.7 reveal that the use of *in* across the six degrees of equivalence is different from each other. As shown by the comparisons of means across the six degrees of equivalence, the use of *in* is observed to decrease gradually as degrees of equivalence move from full to zero. More specifically, the mean reaches the peak at Equivalence I (0.874) and then decreases in a linear manner with the reduction in degrees of equivalence. For Equivalence V where there is zero equivalence in categorization, the mean falls to the lowest point (0.375), but finally it goes up slightly at Equivalence VI.

Besides a linear decrease, three more striking findings are that: (1) As the degree of cross-linguistic equivalence drops from Equivalence I to Equivalence II, there is a significant decrease in the use of *in*; (2) As the degrees of equivalence fall to Equivalence III, there is a more considerable decrease; (3) From Equivalence III, the use of *in* varies moderately.

Table 6.7 ***Descriptive Statistics for the Effect of Degrees of Equivalence***

Degree of equivalence	Mean	Standard deviation	N
Equivalence I	0.874	0.128	150
Equivalence II	0.777	0.177	
Equivalence III	0.450	0.249	
Equivalence IV	0.448	0.293	
Equivalence V	0.375	0.190	
Equivalence VI	0.405	0.231	

Results of ANOVA test in Table 6.8 show that the difference in the use of *in* across the six degrees of equivalence is significant, which confirms that degrees of cross-linguistic equivalence in categorization have a significant effect on the participants' use of *in*, $F(5, 735) = 167.373$, $p = 0.000 < 0.05$.

Table 6.8 ***Results of ANOVA Test for the Effect of Degrees of Equivalence***

Source	SS	Df	Mean Square	F	Sig.
Degree of Equivalence	34.287	5	6.857	167.373	0.000
Error	30.144	735	0.041		

The pairwise comparisons as shown in Table 6.9 further indicate that the significant difference in the use of *in* is observed mainly (1) between Equivalence I and all other degrees of equivalence; (2) between Equivalence II and all other degrees of equivalence; (3) between Equivalence III and Equivalence V. This once again demonstrates that significant changes in the use of *in* mainly occur as the degrees of equivalence fall from full equivalence to partial equivalence.

Table 6.9 ***Pairwise Comparisons of the Use of in across Six Degrees of Equivalence***

Prototypical Context	I	II	III	IV	V	VI
I		0.097*	0.424*	0.426*	0.499*	0.469*
II	−0.097*		0.327*	0.329*	0.402*	0.372*
III	−0.424*	−0.327*		0.002	0.075*	0.045
IV	−0.426*	−0.329*	−0.002		0.073	0.043
V	−0.499*	−0.402*	−0.075*	−0.073		−0.030
VI	−0.469*	−0.372*	−0.045	−0.043	0.030	

In summary, the statistical analysis shows that degrees of equivalence have a significant effect on participants' responses and as degrees of equivalence drop, participants' preference for *in* decreases linearly. In addition, broadly speaking, from Equivalence III the use of *in* does not change significantly.

6.3.2 Use of *in* across Different Proficiency Groups

The effect of L2 proficiency on the use of *in* reported by the statistical analysis includes the main effect of L2 proficiency and the interaction effect of L2 proficiency and degrees of equivalence. Descriptive statistics for the use of *in* across three proficiency groups are reported by Table 6.10. Table 6.11 presents results of ANOVA test of the main effect and the interaction effect. Table 6.12 shows the results of post hoc (Scheffe) test which is performed to find out where the significant difference lies in the use of *in* between each pair of groups. The section ends with Figure 6.2, which depicts the changes of the effect of degrees of equivalence with increasing L2 proficiency.

Descriptive statistics in Table 6.10 illustrate that for each degree of equivalence, the participants' responses are different across the three groups. Except Equivalence III, the use of *in* for each degree of equivalence increases as L2 proficiency improves. For Equivalence III, the mean for IG is lower than that for LG (0.379<0.380). This results in a U-shaped variation in the use of *in* across the three proficiency groups. Besides the U-shaped variation, it can also be seen that while the mean of HG at each degree of equivalence is much higher than that of other two groups, the use of *in* by HG across degrees of equivalence also exhibits a gradual decrease as degrees of equivalence decline

(Figure 6. 2).

The results of the ANOVA test in Table 6. 11 indicate that L2 proficiency has a significant main effect on the participants' use of *in* for each degree of equivalence, $F(2, 735) = 27.330$, $p = 0.000 < 0.05$; to put it another way, the difference in the use of *in* across the groups mentioned above reaches the significant level. The results of post hoc (Scheffe) tests in Table 6. 12 specify that the difference is significant between each pair of proficiency groups.

Table 6. 10 ***Descriptive Statistics for the Effect of Degrees of Equivalence across Three Proficiency Groups***

Equivalence	Proficiency	Mean	Standard deviation	N
1	High	0. 939	0. 067	50
	Intermediate	0. 911	0. 094	50
	Low	0. 773	0. 144	50
2	High	0. 808	0. 156	50
	Intermediate	0. 784	0. 148	50
	Low	0. 740	0. 215	50
3	High	0. 592	0. 244	50
	Intermediate	0. 379	0. 233	50
	Low	0. 380	0. 210	50
4	High	0. 565	0. 236	50
	Intermediate	0. 440	0. 293	50
	Low	0. 340	0. 306	50
5	High	0. 432	0. 221	50
	Intermediate	0. 347	0. 159	50
	Low	0. 346	0. 175	50
6	High	0. 440	0. 255	50
	Intermediate	0. 430	0. 220	50
	Low	0. 345	0. 208	50

Table 6. 11 ***Results of ANOVA Test of the Effect of L2 Proficiency***

Source	SS	Df	Mean Square	F	Sig.
Proficiency	0. 509	2	0. 254	27. 300	0. 000
Equivalence * Proficiency	1. 161	10	0. 116	2. 833	0. 002
Error	30. 144	735	0. 041		

Table 6. 12 ***Scheffe Test Results of the Difference in the Use of in between Groups***

Proficiency	High	Intermediate	Low
High		0. 0805*	0. 1422*
Intermediate	−0. 0805*		0. 0617*
Low	−0. 1422*	−0. 0617*	

* The mean difference is significant at the 0. 05 level.

Apart from the main effect, the interaction effect is also reported to be significant, F (10, 735) =2. 833, p=0. 002<0. 05. This means that the effect of degrees of equivalence on the use of *in* varies with L2 proficiency. Figure 6. 2 provides a more visual description of the interaction effect. As shown in Figure 6. 2, the interaction between L2 proficiency and degrees of equivalence manifests itself mainly in the following two aspects:

Firstly, for IG, the effect of Equivalence III on the use of *in* is weakened with the mean of Equivalence III being lower than that of Equivalence VI.

Secondly, for LG, the use of *in* at Equivalence IV falls to the lowest; in other words, the least frequent use of *in* by LG is not observed in the case of zero equivalence, but in the case of partial equivalence.

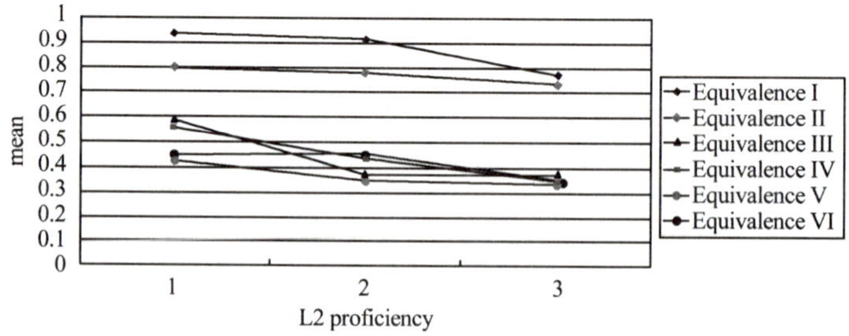

Figure 6. 2 Interaction between L2 Proficiency and Degrees of Equivalence

To recapitulate, the statistical analysis indicates that L2 proficiency has a significant main effect on the participants' use of *in*, and with the exception of Equivalence III, the number of *in* goes up with the improvement of L2 proficiency. The interaction effect is also reported to be significant.

6.4 Discussion of the Results

In the above section, the statistical analysis shows that both prototypicality and degrees of equivalence have significant effect on participants' use of *in* and the interactions between the two factors and L2 proficiency are also significant. In this section, the researcher will make an in-depth discussion on the results with the intent to find empirical evidence for the hypothesis about the cognitive underpinnings of the use of *in* by L2 learners and their developmental changes formulated in Chapter Three. Based on the discussions, the conceptual mechanism of L1 transfer in Chinese EFL learners' use of *in* will be revealed.

6.4.1 Cognitive Basis of the Use of *in* by L2 Learners

In Chapter Three, within the framework of Langacker's (1987) valence theory and connectionist accounts of bilingual conceptual representation (Finkbeiner 2002), it is hypothesized that L2 learners' use of *in* is under the influence of both prototypicality and degrees of equivalence. The findings of the significant effects of both prototypicality and degrees of equivalence support the hypothesis and indicate both of the factors play an important role in defining the elaborative distance between the schematic landmark profiled by *in* and the specific object concept profiled by the noun; to put it another way, they constitute the cognitive basis of the use of *in* by L2 learners. This finding in turn provides cross-linguistic evidence for Langacker's valence theory by illustrating the conceptual dependency of the use of *in* on the two systems of categorization and simultaneously supports the assumption that bilingual conceptual representation is a compound consisting of language-specific features and features shared by the two languages.

However, the results of how the two factors exert effect reveal that degrees of cross-linguistic equivalence override prototypicality in defining the elaborative distance; to be precise, how well the two languages converge in construing containers is more important in motivating L2 learners' use of *in*. The overriding influence of degrees of equivalence is mainly evident in how the participants' use of *in* varies across seven prototypical contexts and six degrees of cross-linguistic equivalence.

6.4.1.1 Variation across Prototypical Contexts

The first evidence for the more contribution of degrees of equivalence is the non-linear variation of participants' use of *in* across seven prototypical contexts. As revealed in Section 6.2, participants' preference for *in* does not decrease as prototypicality of containers declines. L1-based prototype concept has been noted to affect the use of *in* by monolingual English natives. As prototypicality of the container denoted by the nominal predicate increases, the possibility of the combination between the noun and *in* increases. But this is not found in participants' use of *in*. Though *in* is most preferred with Type I container, the least preference is not observed with Type VII, but with Type II.

Besides the non-linear variation, the use of *in* in each prototypical context is found to be influenced by degrees of cross-linguistic equivalence in construing the containers involved in this context. As reported above, compared with Types II, III and V, Types I, IV, VI and VII elicit more instances of *in*. Pairwise comparisons further illustrate that the difference in means between each pair of the former group (I, IV, VI and VII) or between each pair of the latter group (II, III and V) is not significant. This might be attributed to their diversity in degrees of equivalence. In the light of the two classificatory frameworks of containers in terms of prototypicality and degrees of cross-linguistic equivalence in categorization, English and Chinese speakers tend to be more equivalent in construing Types I, IV, VI and VII than in Types II, III and V. Take Type VII as an example. As the most peripheral member, it has the greatest distance from the prototype. However, the similar perceptual experience (e.g. the located object moves within the area delimited by the reference object) motivates both English and Chinese speakers to construe this type of objects as an instance of CONTAINER with the manipulation of mental closure and conceptual projection from the three-dimensional configuration to the one-dimensional configuration (Hottenroth 1993: 210). Such convergence in categorization shortens the elaborative distance.

Another example is provided by the significant difference in the use of *in* between Type V and Type VI. Interlingually speaking, there tends to be more equivalence in construing Type VI containers. For instance,

(105) 宇宙里的中子星
yuzhou li de zhongzi xing
Universe in De neutron star
'the neutron star in the universe' (CCLC)

However, more differences are identified in the construal of Type V containers. For example,

(106) the car in the square (BNC)

(107) 广场上的汽车
guangchang shang de qiche
square on De_1 car
'the car in the square' (CCLC)

While *guang chang li* is also acceptable in Chinese, it is much less frequently used than *guang chang shang* with a frequency ratio of 26 : 2346 as shown in CCLC. This indicates the square is more likely to be construed as a supporting surface rather than a container in Chinese. As a result, in the item "there is a car ________ the square", 91 participants select *on/over* to complete the sentence, whereas in the item "there are black holes ________ the universe", only four participants use *on*. Participants' Chinese translation "*guang chang shang*" also confirms the influence of L1-based categorization of the square. Therefore, though Type V containers are less prototypical than Type VI by being bounded in space, the lower degree of equivalence lengthens the elaborative distance.

In addition, the finding that the lowest frequency of *in* occurs in Prototypical Contexts II and III also supports the constraint of degrees of equivalence on the effect of prototypicality. In construing Type II containers that are considerably open (e. g., fork, stirrup) and Type III containers, there tends to be zero equivalence between the two languages. For instance,

(108) The pulpit cried in the pulpit.
牧师在布道台上哭起来了。(GCEPC)

(109) Here was a memory hole in the opposite wall.
对面墙上有个忘怀洞。(GCEPC)

In terms of prototypicality, the pulpit is an instance of Type II containers by being three-dimensional, half-open, hollow and discrete, but in terms of equivalence, it is a marginal type because *bu dao tai li* is unacceptable in Chinese at all. To be precise, *bu dao tai* is construed as an instance of SUPPORTING SURFACE rather than CONTAINER in Chinese. Such zero equivalence causes 99 participants to use *on* in the item "there is a priest ______ the pulpit". Obviously this erroneous expansion of the semantic category of *on* results from the negative transfer of L1-based construal of the conceptual content of the noun *pulpit*.

Of the seven prototypical contexts, the highest frequency of *in* is found in Prototypical Context I. The combination between strong prototypicality and high degree of equivalence makes the elaborative distance shortest. This finding bears resemblance to Correa-Beningfield's (1985) finding of the positive transfer in Spanish-speaking learners' use of *in*: the correspondence in prototype between *in* and its Spanish equivalent *en* facilitated learners' correct choice of *in*. Similar views were found in Ma (2007) who stated that the similarity between English and Chinese in assigning the core semantic members would ease the learning of English spatial prepositions.

Taken together, it might be reasonably assumed that the effect of equivalence inhibits the effect of prototypicality in motivating the use of *in*.

6.4.1.2 Variation across Degrees of Equivalence

The second evidence supporting the overriding influence of degrees of equivalence is related to the variation in the use of *in* across the six degrees of equivalence.

Different from the variation of participants' responses across prototypical contexts, the variation of responses across degrees of equivalence is a linear one. As shown in Section 6.3, participants' preference for *in* with Equivalence I is the strongest and with the two types of zero equivalence, the use of *in* falls to the lowest point. This indicates the use of *in* is more subject to the change of degrees of equivalence in categorization rather than prototypicality of containers.

Following Sense Model (Finkbeiner 2002), for bilingual learners, especially beginners, there is a representational asymmetry (Finkbeiner 2002: 153) between the translation equivalents. The conceptual structure underlying the use of a L2 form mainly consists of L1-based conceptual features. Therefore, it might be assumed that the more convergent the two languages are in categorization, the more likely *in* is activated. The finding as to the linear increase of the use of *in* with rising cross-linguistic equivalence in categorization supports the hypothesis.

A closer look at the results reveals that significant changes in the use of *in* mainly occurs at the first three degrees of equivalence. For Equivalence I where English and Chinese converge fully in object concept, participants' preference for *in* hits the peak and is significantly stronger than that for other degrees of equivalence. In the case of full conceptual equivalence, learning a new L2 word is greatly simplified as a process of learning to say in the other way (MacWhinney 2007: 80); in other words, learners do not bother to modify the patterns of linkage among the conceptual features related to the preposition *in* but rather map the previously built concept of spatial containment directly onto *in* without making errors. With the positive influence of full conceptual equivalence, the senses that reflect such conceptual equivalence are usually acquired much earlier than other senses. And in addition, containers involved in this degree of equivalence are mainly from Type I and Type VII, thus the most frequent use of *in* with Equivalence I provides further support for the overriding influence of degrees of cross-linguistic equivalence on the participants' use of *in*.

In the case of Equivalence II, the frequency of *in* suffered a significant decrease. For this typological context, the construal of containers in Chinese alternates between CONTAINER and other categories in accordance with the perspectives taken by the viewers, but similar to English, CONTAINER is given more priority in Chinese. Despite the similarity, the acceptability of other spatial categories still causes learners to opt for other prepositions. Take the following item as an example.

(110) He is walking ________ the rain.

As shown in learner data, besides *in*, the other two prepositions *under* and *below* are also preferred by the participants. In accordance with CCLC, the Chinese expression *yu xia* is of much lower frequency than *yu zhong/yu li* (frequency ratio: 19 : 3040), but it is also acceptable in Chinese. This means the object concept profiled by the noun *yu* might also be construed as a specification of the schematic landmark profiled by the spatial expression *xia*. For instance,

(111) ……在雨下漫游。

zai *yu* *xia* *manyou*

at rain under wander

"... wander in the rain". (CCLC)

The preferential choice of the English equivalents of *xia* demonstrates the negative influence from L1-based construal of the reference object. Additionally, semantic confusion between *below* and *under* is also observed here. This is attributed to the cross-linguistic difference in the distinctions of categories. The spatial relationship represented by Chinese expression *xia* splits into more than one category in English that is related to different prepositions. As such, an appropriate use of the prepositions presupposes an internalization of the finer distinctions specific to English (Pavlenko 2009: 138) by Chinese learners of English.

The alternation between the CONTAINER category and other categories causes a reduction in the use of *in* by learners, but the positive effect is still strong with the frequency of *in* of Equivalence II being significantly higher than that of other typological contexts. This suggests that convergence in identifying CONTAINER as a more typical category between English and Chinese leads the majority of participants to the establishment of the similarity between English and Chinese in categorization.

On the whole, in the case of Equivalence I and Equivalence II, *in* is mostly correctly used by participants. To put it another way, when there is full or near equivalence in conceptualization, L1 will facilitate the acquisition of *in*. This finding is echoed by many studies (Ma 2007; Pavlenko 2009; Zhang & Liu 2013). This can also be explained by Gentner and Bowerman's Typological Prevalence Hypothesis (2009: 467):

> All else being equal, within a given domain, the more frequently a given way of categorizing is found in the languages of the world, the more natural it is for human cognizers, hence the easier it will be for children to learn.

It follows that if a reference object, whether being a prototypical container like the box or a peripheral one like the queue, is conventionally categorized as a container both in English and Chinese, the pattern of categorization would be more cognitively natural to human beings in the way that it fits in with the human's perceptual intuition, therefore, it would be easier for the L2 learners to be internalized.

However, as degrees of equivalence drop from Equivalence II to Equivalence III, the frequency stays low. Pairwise comparisons in the above section specify that except between Equivalence III and Equivalence V, the difference in frequency between other pairs does not reach the significant level. This indicates that as degrees of equivalence decline, the elaborative distance between the schematic container and the object concept profiled by the noun keeps increasing.

As mentioned in Section 4. 3. 2, for Equivalence III, there is similar alternation between the CONTAINER category and other conceptual categories in Chinese, but what distinguishes it from Equivalence II is that the CONTAINER category is less preferred than other categories by Chinese. The effect of Equivalence III on the participants' use of *in* is well illustrated in the following two items.

(112) Let's have a rest ________ the shade.

(113) It is bad for your eyes to read ________ a dim light.

In Chinese the two reference objects are more likely to be construed as a cover or a protector which is vertically higher than the located object and exerts physical force over the located object from above (Tyler & Evans 2003: 121). The analysis of learner data reveals that in the two items, ***under*** occurs 68 times and 67 times respectively. Their Chinese translations provide further support for the transfer from L1. Besides ***under***, ***below*** also occurs 10 times and 5 times respectively. This provides another piece of evidence for the effect of cross-linguistic difference in the distinctions of categories on the use of English prepositions. One of the participants reported that the reason for using *below* instead of *under* was that his middle-school English teacher had ever told him that *under* is akin to *over* which required the reference object to be perpendicular to the located object, yet *below* precluded such perpendicularity. Actually as claimed by Tyler and Evans (2003: 121), the difference between *under* and *below* mainly lies in whether the located object is within the potential reach of the reference object. Obviously, the participants' misuse of the preposition *below* can be classified as an induced error which derives from the faulty explanation of L2 knowledge (Ellis 1999: 60).

Another type of partial equivalence, Equivalence IV, also poses great challenge to the learners in some cases. For example,

(114) He is watching me ________ the rearview mirror.

In this item, only 37 participants use the preposition *in*, whereas the prepositions *through* and *from* occur 84 times and 15 times respectively. As mentioned in Section 4. 3. 2, the Chinese expression *cong*+*N* falls into two categories: *in*+*N* and *from/through*+*N*. Because *cong*+*N* is more equivalent to *from/through*+*N* in form and function, participants show more preference for *through/from*. This indicates that in the case of partial equivalence, a full conceptual equivalence is likely to be assumed by learners on the basis of perceived formal similarity (Ringbom 2006). Similar findings are also reported by Bohnacker and Rosen (2008), Jarvis and Pavlenko (2008) and Wang (2010). This further demonstrates that partial equivalence will also contribute to the lengthening of the elaborative distance.

Finally, the lowest frequency is found in Equivalence V where there is zero equivalence between the two languages in schematization (Talmy 2000). This suggests that the elaborative distance is the longest in this typological context. Take the following item as an example.

(115) There's a boy ________ the tree.

Actually, since the primary school, Chinese learners of English have been exposed to such expressions as *a bird in the tree*. In this item, the word *bird* is replaced by the word *boy*. In accordance with the classification of containers in terms of prototypicality, the tree should be a member of Type II containers. While the reference object is of strong prototypicality, the analysis of learner data reveals that *on* and *up* occur 82 times and 4 times respectively and *in* occurs only 59 times. This means that strong prototypicality does not inhibit or weaken the negative effect of the zero equivalence on the use of *in*. Thus, it might be reasonably assumed that a high degree of cross-linguistic equivalence can inhibit the effect of prototypicality, but not vice versa. More evidence can be found in this item.

(116) There is a nest ________ the fork of the tree.

The four translation equivalents of the Chinese locative expression *shang*, *on*, *over*, *above* and *up* all make their appearance. *On* occurs 101 times, *over* 16 times, *up* 4 times and *above* once. Only 21 participants correctly choose *in*. According to Lv (1999: 471-473), the locative marker *shang* gives special prominence to the fact that one object is vertically higher than the other object to the neglect of the contiguity between the two objects. Besides being a locative marker, *shang* can also be used as a directional verb which refers to the event of moving from a lower position to a higher position. It can be clearly seen that the linguistic category *shang* subsumes the four distinct categories *on*, *over*, *above* and *up*. Thus, the appearance of the four prepositions not only reveals the interference from the language-specific perspective, but also the interference from the cross-linguistic difference in how fine the conceptual distinctions are made. Similar claims were made by Pavlenko who had pointed out that transfer would be particularly apparent in the cases where L1 has a more expanded category (Pavlenko 2009: 135). This shows that the internalization of the fine-grained distinctions particular to the target language is a thorny problem for the learners to handle.

But one more point worth mentioning is that compared with Example (115), this item is observed to be more likely to activate the preposition *over*. As reported by the participants in the interview, the reason for the misuse of *over* mainly lies in that the nest is not in contact with the bottom of the fork but is directly above the fork. According to Tyler and Evans (2003), [one object being vertically higher than the reference object] and [the two objects lacking in contiguity] are two core features in the conceptual representations of *over*. This indicates that learning experience with *over* enables some L2-specific conceptual features to be internalized by learners and directs their attention to the aspects of the object that are highlighted by L2. This provides the empirical support for the hypothesis that L2 learning is a process of conceptual restructuring (Pavlenko 2009: 150) whereby L2-specific conceptual features are gradually involved in the access of English spatial prepositions. Despite the restructuring, the use of *over* is still based on L1-specific construal of the conceptual content of the noun. One important reason might be that in learning of English spatial prepositions, focus is always set on the semantic or conceptual representations of prepositions rather than those of nouns.

Though the frequency of *in* for Equivalence VI which is put at the end of equivalence continuum is not the lowest, the pairwise comparisons indicate the difference between Equivalence V and Equivalence VI does not reach the significant level. This suggests that Equivalence VI also causes considerable trouble to learners. For example,

(117) There are 3 apples ________ the plate.

(118) They are cleaning ________ the campus.

As reported by the participants in the interview, the expression *on the plate* actually was learned in the elementary school. And the collocation between *on* and *campus* had been emphasized by their middle school teachers many times. However, the analysis of learner data reveals that there are 57 and 54 learners misusing *in* respectively. It might be attributed to the difference between English and Chinese in construing the prototype of the two categories CAMPUS and PLATE. In the western culture, campus is usually not enclosed with high walls. The definition of *Random House Webster's Dictionary* also shows that the word *campus* refers to a tract of land for a specific purpose. However, its Chinese translation equivalent *xiao yuan* is conventionally construed as a container, because *yuan* as the head of the structure highlights a walled-in area delimited for the sake of privacy or safety. Bathed in different cultures, learners form different mental images for the CAMPUS category. The misuse of *in* indicates the projection of L1-based prototypical image of CAMPUS onto the word *campus*.

In sum, in the case of full or near equivalence in categorization, the elaborative distance between the schematic container and the conceptual referent profiled by the noun is the shortest and there is the highest possibility of *in*. As degrees of equivalence fall to partial equivalence, the elaborative distance is greatly lengthened and the possibility is in decline. And finally at zero equivalence, the elaborative distance is the longest and the possibility of *in* reaches the lowest point. Following the methodological framework established in Section 5. 6. 2, the diversity in learner data across the typological contexts is an important evidence of L1 transfer. In addition, the comparison of learner data, the comparison between learner data and their L1 data and the comparison between learner data and native data also confirm the occurrence of L1 transfer. This means that the reduction in the use of *in* with the decline of degrees of cross-linguistic equivalence indicates a decrease in positive transfer and an increase in negative transfer from L1. Therefore, it can be said that degrees of cross-linguistic equivalence in categorization of containers constitute the conceptual mechanism facilitating or inhibiting L1 transfer.

In this section a comprehensive description of the variation in learners' preference for *in* across different prototypical contexts and different degrees of equivalence is made on the basis of the results reported in Sections 6. 2 and 6. 3. The finding that both prototypicality and degrees of equivalence have a significant effect on the use of *in* indicates that both of them are involved in defining the elaborative distance between the schematic container and the conceptual referent profiled by the noun. This provides support for the model established in Chapter Three to account for the formation of the construction [IN + N] by L2 learners. But the results of linear variation across different degrees of equivalence and the constraint of degrees of equivalence on the effect of prototypicality suggest that degrees of equivalence override prototypicality in defining the elaborative distance. A high degree of equivalence facilitates the occurrence of L1 positive transfer. As degrees of equivalence decrease, elaborative distance is lengthened and the negative transfer from L1 rises. Based on the above discussion, it might be reasonably assumed that degrees of cross-linguistic equivalence constitute the conceptual mechanism of L1 transfer. But as hypothesized in Chapter Three, the accumulation of L2 experience will push more and more L2-specific conceptual features to be internalized and cause learners' use of *in* to be more conceptually motivated by prototypicality. As a result, conceptual transfer undergoes a gradual reduction with degrees of equivalence giving way to prototypicality in affecting the use of *in*. The next section will be focused on the confirmation of the hypothesized developmental variation of the effects of prototypicality and degrees of equivalence.

6.4.2 The Change of the Effects of Prototypicality and Degrees of Equivalence with L2 Proficiency

The results of the effects of prototypicality and degrees of cross-linguistic equivalence on the use of *in* show that degrees of equivalence are more important in motivating the use of *in* by L2 learners and constitutes the conceptual impetus of L1 transfer. As hypothesized in Chapter three, in the early stage of L2 learning, the use of *in* is more conceptually motivated by degrees of equivalence, but as L2 experience increases, the effect of prototypicality will be strengthened. In the following, a discussion on how the effects of the two factors change with L2 proficiency is made to reveal the cognitive basis underlying the variation of L1 transfer in the use of *in*.

6.4.2.1 The Main Effect of L2 Proficiency

Results of the main effect of L2 proficiency mainly consist of two parts. The first is concerned with the variation in the use of *in* across the three proficiency groups for each degree of equivalence and the second is with the variation in the use of *in* across the three groups for each prototypical context.

Both ANOVA tests and post hoc tests show L2 proficiency has a significant main effect on the use of *in* for each degree of equivalence. Figure 6.2 illustrates that except Equivalence III, participants' use of *in* rises as L2 proficiency increases, or in other words, participants' preference for *in* is closer to that of natives with increasing L2 proficiency. Especially for HG, the use of *in* with each degree of equivalence is much more frequent than that for the other two groups. This suggests that as L2 proficiency increases, there is a gradual reduction of negative conceptual transfer in the use of *in* which provides support to the hypothesized developmental variation in the effect of degrees of cross-linguistic equivalence. To be precise, the increasing exposure to L2 input is contributory to establishing L2-specific patterns of linkage among the features defining the category CONTAINER and to strengthening the connections between spatial concepts and L2 nouns in such a way that learners gradually realize the specifications of L2 lexical concepts and avoid the projection of L1-based categorization onto L2 words.

Another important implication from the developmental variation of conceptual transfer is that the development of L2 proficiency promotes learners to form a proper judgment of cross-linguistic equivalence in categorization which causes them to be susceptible to the differences and thereby avoiding negative transfer of L1. Ringbom (1986: 150) has claimed that in L2 acquisition, learners are primarily concerned with what similarities they can utilize between L2 and L1 to facilitate their L2 learning. The Semantic Equivalence Hypothesis proposed by Ijaz (1986: 448) also points out that the use of L2 words is based on the assumption that L1-mediated patterns of conceptualization and linguistic coding practices serve as the essential criteria for those in the L2. Such assumption is named as "subjective similarity" to distinguish the similarity that learners assume to exist from the similarity that actually exists (Jarvis & Pavlenko 2008: 177). Once learners perceive the relevance of L1 to the present learning task and draw upon it, transfer occurs. If learners' subjective similarity accords with the objective similarity, positive transfer will take place, or else, there will be negative transfer. It has been empirically demonstrated that development in L2 proficiency would facilitate the formation of appropriate judgment of cross-linguistic distance (Kellerman 1979; Zhang & Yu 2011). This is further supported by the finding of the gradual reduction of negative transfer in the use of *in* with the increase in L2 proficiency.

The developmental variation in conceptual transfer is also illustrated by the main effect of L2 proficiency on the use of *in* in each prototypical context. As revealed in Table 6. 4, except Types V and VI, the frequency of *in* increases with advancing L2 proficiency. Also *in* in each prototypical context is significantly more preferred by HG than by the other two groups. This suggests that the improvement of L2 proficiency promotes the development of L2-based construal of containers and strengthens the effect of prototypicality. Similar findings are reported by many conceptual transfer studies (Cook, et al. 2006; Hohenstein, et al. 2006; Malt & Sloman 2003; Jarvis 2011). They all found that increase in L2 experience would cause the weakening of the influence of L1-based conceptualization to some extent. Following connectionism (Ellis 2011, 2013; Wang 2001), the increase in L2 input will lead to the strengthening of L2-mediated links among the conceptual units and the level of activation of L2-specific features will be raised accordingly. Thus, the previously-built conceptual structures related to the CONTAINER category will be restructured and this will result in more involvement of L2-based categorization in defining the elaborative distance. This supports the hypothesized variation of the effect of prototypicality on the use of *in*.

Despite the supports for the developmental variation of conceptual transfer, the strong effect of degrees of equivalence can still be observed in the responses of HG. This is particularly evident in the case of lower degrees of equivalence. Figure 6. 2 shows that while HG shows more preference for *in* than the other two groups, the use of *in* also undergoes a significant reduction as degrees of equivalence decline. For example, in the item "Romantic love is like an oasis ________ the desert", *on* is misused by HG 3 times, whereas in the item "there is a boy ________ the tree", *on* is misused 24 times. Though the tree is more prototypical than the desert, the lower degree of equivalence in categorizing still causes HG to misuse the prepositions from the interference of L1. This suggests that although the effect of prototypicality is strengthened with increasing L2 proficiency, degrees of cross-linguistic equivalence still play an important part in defining the elaborative distance. More precisely, the improvement of L2 proficiency promotes the modification of previously built patterns of categorization with internalization of L2-based concepts and causes a reduction of negative transfer, but it does not lead to the dominance of prototypicality-based categorization which might free learners from the influence of L1-based categorization. Similar claim was made by von Humboldt as early as the 19th century: the escape from the L1 transfer was never completely successful (Odlin 2005: 8). According to the retrospective reports of the participants from HG, ignorance of the conceptual dependence of prepositions on the nominal predicates and a lack of teachers' explicit comparative studies of the English prepositions and their Chinese equivalents at the conceptual level are mainly responsible for the strong effect of degrees of equivalence.

Aside from this, the U-shaped variation observed with Equivalence III and Type V and VI containers also indicates that the improvement of L2 proficiency does not always result in a reduction of conceptual transfer.

As noted in Section 4. 3. 2, the conceptual referents profiled by the English nouns in the case of Equivalence III, alternate between CONTAINER and other categories in Chinese in accordance with the perspectives taken by the viewers, and furthermore, CONTAINER in Chinese is not as prototypical as in English. This means the distance between English and Chinese of Equivalence III is bigger than that of Equivalence II and therefore, it might cause more negative influence than Equivalence II. The most frequent use of *in* by HG shows that the increase in L2 proficiency causes a reduction in negative transfer, but for IG the increasing exposure to L2 does not lead to a decrease but a slight increase in negative transfer. Following the classification of containers in terms of prototypicality, the containers involved in Equivalence III are subsumed within Type V or Type VI containers. Thus the U-shaped pattern of variation observed with Equivalence III corresponds with the variation observed with the two types of containers.

U-shaped L2 learning behavior has been investigated in many L2 acquisition studies (Kellerman 1979; Lightbown 1985, 2000; McLaughlin 1990; Wei 2012) and stimulated a wide spectrum of explanations for the non-linear developmental sequence. For example, Lightbown (1985: 177) pointed out:

> Having practiced a particular form or pattern does not mean that the form or pattern is permanently established. Learners appear to forget forms and structures which they had seemed previously to master and which they had extensively practiced.

Another notable account is from McLaughlin's notion of restructuring (1990). As McLaughlin claimed, restructuring, a term borrowed from developmental psychology, refers to the qualitative changes in learners' internal representations of L2 knowledge, which mainly include:

(1) The changes from the exemplar-bound representations to rule-bound representations as reported in the studies of L2 morphological development (Ellis & Schmidt 1997; Li 2002), in which learners at the intermediate level are found to commit more errors than beginners with the overgeneralization of morphological rules;

(2) The changes from L1-based conceptual representations to L2-based representations in L2 semantic development, which were well illustrated in Kellerman's (1979) study of Dutch-speaking learners' acceptability judgment of the transitive and intransitive uses of the English word *break*, in which learners of more L2 learning experience were found to be more likely to reject

intransitive uses of *break* with their increasing awareness of the functional distinctions between the two types of uses that were not present in Dutch;

(3) The changes from formulaic speech to creative speech with gradual extraction of rules from chunks as demonstrated in the study of L2 developmental sequence of negation (Lightbown & Spada 1999), in which learners at the initial stage of SLA were observed to use the negative structures, like *I don't know*, correctly as memorized chunks, then with the unpacking of the formulaic speech into discrete constituents motivated by new L2 input, they were found to produce incorrect negative structures, like *she don't understand*.

From the information processing perspective, the main impetus for the restructuring is new L2 input that cannot be handled by learners' current knowledge of L2 (McLaughlin 1990: 120). In the process of restructuring, learners' performance may be less target-like than earlier, but it reflects learner's ability to use language creatively beyond "mimicking or living off the L1" (Lightbown 2000: 442).

Following the above claims, an attempt is made to analyze what might lie behind the U-shaped behavior in the present study. As noted in Section 4.2.2, Type V containers are characterized as two-dimensional, clearly bounded and discrete objects. On the one hand, the presence of the attribute "two-dimensionality" causes this type of containers to be not very representative of the category. On the other hand, the objects of this type are more likely to be construed as instances of the category SUPPORTING SURFACE in Chinese. A comparison of learner data between LG and IG reveals that lower frequency of *in* for IG mainly occurs in the following two items.

(119) He made some notes ________ the margin.

(120) There's a cow ________ the field.

In Example (119), *in* is correctly used by 9 participants from IG and 26 participants from LG. The follow-up interview with the participants from the two groups shows that the participants from the middle school have been instructed about the semantic distinction between *in the margin* and *on the margin* and they have committed the expression *in the margin* to their memory as a chunk. As a consequence, there are only 3 instances of *on* in LG as opposed to 11 times in IG. This indicates that the negative transfer might be inhibited by teachers' explicit instructions and rote learning. The participants at the intermediate level also acknowledged that they had learnt the expression in middle school, but with time passing by and the reduction of intensive grammar training, the teachers' instructions and the chunk *in the margin* were gradually dismissed from memory. This accords with Lightbown's account.

However, a striking finding is that the preposition most preferred by the intermediate participants is not *on* but *by* which occurs 21 times as against 3 times in LG. The composite structure *by the margin* is neither in the L1 nor in the L2 and therefore, it might be treated as a result of learners' restructuring. As revealed in the interview, learners seem to be misled by the Chinese equivalent *ye bian*, especially the Chinese form *bian*. Actually, *by* is used to indicate a spatial relationship in which the located object and the reference object are close to each other on the horizontal plane (Lindstromberg, 1997: 141). The difference among the three prepositions *by*, *on* and *in* is well illustrated by Examples (121)-(123).

(121) Victorine tossed them into the plastic waste bowl that stood by the side of the sink.

(122) He relapsed into grim gloom and stood on the side of the bath in his white T-shirt.

(123) This man succeeded in cutting a hole in the side of the carriage. (BNC)

The differences among the three prepositions, as demonstrated in Figure 6.3, can be summarized as follows: (1) For *by*, the close physical proximity on the horizontal plane between the side and the bowl is highlighted but the geometrical attributes of the side are neglected; (2) Concerning *in*, little attention is paid to the vertical or horizontal relation between the side and the hole, but the attributes that define the side as a container are emphasized; (3) Unlike *by* and *in*, in the conceptual structure of *on*, equal importance is attached to the direction and the geometrical attributes, specifically speaking, *on* initially differs from *by* in that it refers to the vertical spatial closeness between the side and the man; secondly it differs from *in* in that the schematic landmark profiled by *on* is a supporting surface rather than a container.

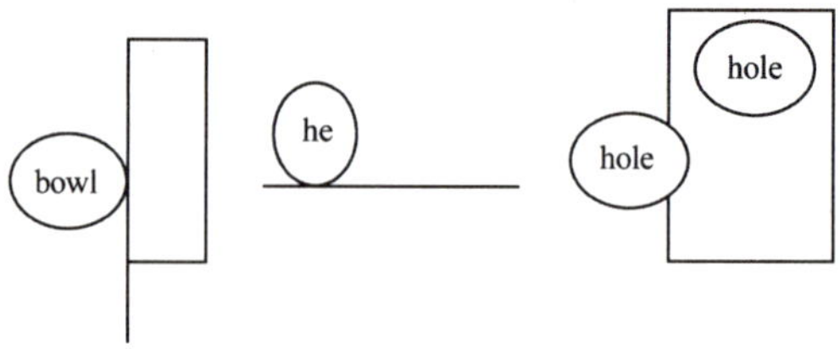

Figure 6. 3 Differences in Conceptual Representations among *by*, *on* and *in*

According to *Random House Webster's Dictionary*, the word *margin* refers to [the space around the printed or written matter on a page], or in other words, an area in which the notes are located. Therefore, *in* is preferred over *on* and *by*. In short, the misuse of *by* is mainly attributed to the assumed equivalence between *margin* and *bian* and the resultant confusion of semantic categories between *by* and *in*.

The comparison of learner data between the two groups in Example (120) reveals 36 instances of *in* in LG as opposed to 21 instances in IG, and the instances of *on* in LG are only half of the instances in IG (frequency ratio: 14 : 28). As reported in the interview, overgeneralization of the chunk *in the field* (meaning within a province or department of study or activity) *by* LG contributes to the high frequent use of *in* and thereby effectively inhibiting the interference of L1-based categorization. The participants' Chinese translations of the sentence also show that the reference object field tends to be construed as a supporting surface. This confirms the occurrence of conceptual transfer from the L1. But unlike Example (119), the reason for the stronger transfer effect on IG is not that they forget the chunk but that more experience with the expression *in the field* causes the intermediate learners to become sensitized to the metaphoric use of the expression in such a way that they are more conservative on the choice of *in*. And simultaneously more experience with the form *field* causes them to realize *on the field* is also acceptable in English. This strengthens the previously-built links among the conceptual features that contribute to the construal of the field as a supporting face and encourages the occurrence of conceptual transfer. This provides evidence for one of Andersen's principles for transferrability of L1: "L2 input provides an inducement to generalization from LI" (Andersen 1983, cited in Kellerman 1995: 12).

Actually, the conceptual representation of the *field* in *on the field*, is similar to that of the Chinese expression *chang di* which refers to a piece of land devoted to sports, battles and the like. In this case, the functional zone of the field is more likely to be fixed on the surface of the land on which the located objects stand or move. As such, the field will be categorized as a supporting surface, corresponding with the schematic landmark profiled by *on*. But the learners fail to make a distinction of the conceptual representation between the two instances of *field*.

One interesting finding is that if there is no chunk to resort to, the use of *in* by LG is not more frequent than the use of *in* by IG. For example,

(124) There is a car ________ the square.

The two objects square and field are physically similar to each other and both are more likely to be categorized as a two-dimensional surface corresponding with the landmark profiled by the preposition *on*. Furthermore, there is no chunk (e. g. , in the field or in the margin) to resort to in this item. The comparison of learner data between the two groups reveals that *on* is used by IG 25 times and LG 31 times and *over* is used by IG 5 times and LG once. This indicates without a chunk LG has no advantage over IG in resisting the negative transfer from L1. In addition, more misuse of *over* by IG provides another evidence for the creative use of L2 resulting from learners' restructuring of L2 knowledge. From their translations, four participants interpret the sentence as *There is a car crossing the square* and one interprets it as *There is a car across the square*. One of the participants reported in the interview:

> ...The reason that I chose *over* was that I thought it was similar to the sentences like 'there is a desk over there', or 'go over the street'...The meaning of the sentence might be that the car is in the square that is in the opposite side.

Obviously, the participant assigns the sense [the opposite side] to *over* on the basis of her previous L2 learning experience. However, it might be due to the limited exposure or a lack of explicit instruction of the spatial concepts represented by *over* that the participants tend to confuse *over* with *across*. Following Finkbeiner (2013) who made a fine-grained distinction between *over* and *across* at the conceptual level, the differences between the two prepositions are: (1) As a static preposition, the relational schema profiled by *over* is that the located object is in vertical alignment with the reference object, whereas, the relational schema profiled by *across* is that one object is located opposite to the reference object; (2) As a dynamic preposition, both *over* and *across* can be used to refer to the movement of a located object from one side to the other side, but in the conceptual structure of *over*, the fact that the reference object is above the ground level or is an obstacle to overcome tends to be highlighted. Their difference is well illustrated by the following two figures:

Figure 6.4 Schematic Landmarks Profiled by *over* and *across*

The misuse of *over* again confirms the significant involvement of L2-based spatial conceptualization in learners' use of spatial prepositions and simultaneously provides another evidence for the creative use of L2 resulting from the restructuring of L2 knowledge representation as claimed in the theory of interlanguage. With the exposure to the expressions like *go over the street* or *walk over the bridge*, learners might presume that the spatial schemata profiled by *over* is not just confined to the vertical relationship but also involves such spatial relationship as one object being located opposite to the reference object.

In the case of Type VI containers, the lower frequency of *in* by IG in comparison with LG is mainly evident in the following item:

(125) The African countries decide to build strong institutions ________ a united continent.

The comparison of learner data between IG and LG reveals that the former shows more preference for the preposition *across* in face of the two-dimensional objects extending unboundedly in space. There are 14 instances of *across* in IG, whereas in LG, there are 3 instances of *across*. The interview with the three intermediate learners reveals that their previous exposure to the expressions like *across the country* or *across the world* is the big drive for their overuse of *across*. For them, there is an assumed equivalence between *a united continent* and *the country* or *the world*. The participants believe that what the sentence wants to express is that they would build the institutions stretching throughout the continent and that the preposition *in* evidently is less precise in describing such a spatial relation.

Clearly, the previous learning experience causes learners to internalize a core feature defining the semantic category of *across*: [the located objects stretching from one side of the reference objects to the other side]. This results in the restructuring of the knowledge representation of L2 spatial coding system, which promotes the learners to form a more complex conceptualization of the spatial context and to be more conscious about the verbal specification. To put it another way, they would like to seek for a word that is assumed to be more exact in describing the spatial relationship. This is empirically supported by the studies concerned with the vocabulary development of L2 learners (Li 2002; Laufer 2010) which found that the increase in vocabulary breadth, especially the experience with infrequent words is contributory to deepening their understanding of L2 text and to facilitating the use of infrequent words. However, the development of vocabulary breadth does not guarantee an appropriate use of the word. As revealed by BNC, the nouns collocating with *across* tend to be definite nouns, namely, the nouns that are modified by the definite articles. According to the cognitive analysis of the semantic structure of *across* by Talmy (2000: 192, 195), the schematic landmark profiled by *across* is characterized as a bounded plane. Thus when the object denoted by the noun is unbounded, there tends to be a definite article to modify it. However, in this context the noun *continent* is preceded by the indefinite article. This indicates the conceptual content of *continent* is not equivalent to that of *country* or *world* in the expression *across the country* or *across the world*. Evidently, learners are ignorant of such a difference and make an overgeneralization error. It can be seen that while, following the classificatory framework of errors formulated by Richards (Ellis 1999: 59), overgeneralization errors are identified as intralingual errors, transfer also has a role to play in the overuse of the preposition *across*. Specifically speaking, the cross-linguistic difference in verbalizing the concept of definiteness and indefiniteness between Chinese and English might cause learners to be insensitive to the conceptual distinction between using and non-using of the definite article. As a result, while reading the sentence, learners are likely to have conscious access only to the expansion of the continent, disregarding the attribute of indefiniteness represented by the indefinite article *a*.

Taken together, the reasons for the U-shaped frequency variation mentioned in the above might be as follows: (1) The learners forget the formulaic structures which they have extensively practiced and learned by rote in the middle school; (2) The increase in vocabulary size brings about some changes in the previously built conceptual representations and leads IG to a more complex representation of the spatial context, which causes them to avoid using the preposition *in* or *on*, but to choose the spatial prepositions which they assume would be more precise in verbalizing the geometrical features of the objects; (3) The exposure to a new spatial expression that is similar to Chinese in the pattern of collocation, like *on the field* and *tian ye shang*, promotes the occurrence of L1 transfer. Thus, the above analysis not only confirms some accounts for the U-shaped L2 behavior proposed by McLaughlin and Lightbown, but also sheds some new light on the factors causing the non-linear variation of conceptual transfer. Additionally, an important implication for English teaching in China can be drawn: Vocabulary learning involves much more than memorization of chunks and advancement in vocabulary breadth.

To summarize, the main effects of L2 proficiency on the participants' use of *in* with each prototypical context and each degree of equivalence show that there is gradual reduction of conceptual transfer with more involvement of prototypicality in motivating the use of *in* as L2 proficiency improves. But the finding that HG also suffers much from negative transfer in the case of lower degrees of equivalence demonstrates that degrees of cross-linguistic equivalence are still more decisive in defining the elaborative distance. And finally, when the CONTAINER category splits into more than one category in Chinese and when the containers are two dimensional, IG are more prone to the influence of L1-based categorization.

6.4.2.2 The Interaction between L2 Proficiency and Prototypicality and Degrees of Equivalence

The interaction effect in the present research mainly involves how the effect of prototypicality or the effect of degrees of equivalence vary with the change of L2 proficiency. Results of the interaction effect include results of the variation in the use of *in* by each proficiency group across the seven prototypical contexts and results of the variation of *in* by each group across the six degrees of equivalence.

The interaction effect of L2 proficiency and prototypicality is firstly observed in HG. To be precise, both of the variation across Types I, IV, VI and VII and the variation across Types II and III, exhibit a linear decrease as degrees of prototypicality decline. As mentioned in Section 6. 4. 1. 1, among Types I, IV, VI and VII, there are more similarities in the CONTAINER category between English and Chinese, whereas between Type II and III more instances of zero equivalence in categorization are found. This suggests that when the prototypical contexts are of similar degree of cross-linguistic equivalence, prototypicality will exert a significant effect on participants' use of *in* and inhibit the effect of equivalence. Thus, as prototypicality declines across Types I, IV, VI and VII, the use of *in* decreases gradually. So does the use of *in* across Types II and III with prototypicality going down from Type II to Type III. This provides evidence for the effect of prototypicality on the use of *in* by HG. However, if all the contexts are taken into consideration, the variation does not show a linear decrease with declining prototypicality. This implies even HG who has nine-year formal English learning does not succeed in developing an English-specific prototoypicality-based categorization underlying the use of *in*. Consequently, the use of *in* is still largely dependent on degrees of cross-linguistic equivalence. The effect of prototypicality shows up when the prototypical contexts are of similar degrees of equivalence and when learners are at advanced level of L2 proficiency. In this case, negative transfer from L1 decreases with the rise in prototypicality of containers.

Secondly, the finding that Type I containers do not elicit LG's most frequent use of *in* indicates the effect of prototypicality is inhibited by low L2 proficiency. Analysis of learner data shows that the beginners' assumed similarity between the English prepositions and their Chinese equivalents as listed in the textbook or dictionaries might account for reduced use of *in* in the most prototypical context. The assumed similarity is firstly evident in the miscollocation of the preposition *at* with the common nouns, like *cage*, *bottle* or *telephone box*. Their use of *li* in Chinese translations shows that the reference objects are still largely construed as containers. As revealed in the follow-up interview, the reasons for the misuse of *at* might be boiled down to two points. The first one is concerned with the assumed equivalence between *at and the Chinese preposition zai*. To be precise, influenced by the dictionaries or textbooks, learners tend to treat *zai* as the equivalent of the English preposition *at*. This subjective similarity is strengthened by the fact that the composite structure [*zai* + N] can also be used to denote spatial containment with the omission of the locative marker *li* in some contexts (Chu 2010: 79; Cui 2002: 4). For example,

(126) 我在第一页做了标记。

wo	*zai*		*diyiye*	*zuo*	*le*	*biaoji.*
i	at	the	first page	do	le-ACTL	mark

'I made a mark on the first page'. (CCLC)

This might cause the learners to assume that *at* could be used in English in the same way. However, limited L2 exposure prevents some learners of LG from realizing that such cross-linguisitic overlap occurs only when *at* collocates with the nouns referring to the geopolitical areas (e. g. , *park* or *city*). The second one is concerned with the nonspecific reference of *at*. Compared with *in* and *on*, *at*, with the landmark schematized as a zero-dimensional point, is less specific in characterizing the spatial relationship between the objects (Herskovits 1986; Lindstromberg 1997; Wu & Wei 2007). Therefore, some learners believe it might be safer to choose *at* when they are confused. Similar findings were reported by Young-Davy (2000: 211). In his study of the Japanese-speaking learners' acquisition of English spatial prepositions, he found when L2 makes finer linguistic distinctions than L1 and when learners could not fully comprehend their differences, the learners tend to choose a preposition that indicates the nonspecific reference.

Another example for the misleading of the assumed similarity is found in the misuse of the preposition *from* in the following two items.

(127) Listen to the noises ________ the classroom.

(128) I see ________ your eyes that you know I can do nothing else.

It can be clearly seen that the learners map L1 concept represented by the expression *cong* + *N* + *li* (*zhong*) onto L2 expression *from*+ *N*. As shown in the comparisons of the differences in the CONTAINER category between English and Chinese in Chapter Four, the linguistic category *cong* + *N* + *li* falls into two categories in English: *in* + *N* and *from/through* + N. For example,

(129) I could see Mac watching me in his rearview mirror.
我能看见迈克正从后视镜里望着我。

(130) I looked through crevices in the pailings.
我从篱笆缝里往里看。

(131) Seen thus, from the pure and frosty darkness in which he stood, it seemed to be seething in a mist of heat.
从他立足的洁净寒冷的黑地里看过去,这个屋子好像在热雾当中沸腾。(GCEPC)

It can be seen that there is more correspondence between *cong* + *N* and *from/through* + *N*, because both can refer to a fictive motion event and both of the nouns are construed as a container serving as a path, but for *in* + *N*, a factual perception event is profiled and the noun is construed as a container. More importantly, *cong* is usually the translation equivalent of *from/through* provided by dictionaries and textbooks. As stated by Ringbom (2006), L2 beginners tend to assume one-to-one relationship rather than one-to-many or many-to-one relationship between translation equivalents. In addition, they are ready to assume full equivalence between the two items that are formally similar to each other, neglecting their partial divergence in the conceptual representations. Thus, with one-to-one correspondence established between *from/through* and *cong*, the nouns are construed as the containers serving as the path and motivate the production of *from/through*.

The above instances of inappropriate replacement of the preposition *in* with other prepositions well illustrate that if there are no chunks to memorize, the beginners are more ready to establish full equivalence between the translation equivalents, especially the equivalents that just partially overlap with each other. Such overgeneralized subjective similarity leads to the occurrence of negative transfer even in the most prototypical context. This provides hard evidence for little effect of prototypicality on the use of *in* at the early stage of L2 learning.

Apart from the interaction between L2 proficiency and prototypicality, the effect of degrees of equivalence also change with L2 proficiency.

Firstly, IG's use of *in* with Equivalence III is less frequent than their use of *in* with Equivalence VI where there is zero equivalence in categorization between English and Chinese. As noted in the above section, for IG who are at a stage of knowledge restructuring is more conservative in transferring L1 knowledge to L2 (Kellerman 1979). The reference objects within Equivalence III are put into the CONTAINER category and other categories as well in Chinese. With conscious avoidance of L1 transfer, they tend to choose the prepositions that are assumed to be L2-specific, like the production of the composite structure *over the fork*, *over the square* or *by the margin*. This indicates that there has been some involvement of L2-based spatial concepts in the production of English spatial prepositions. However, their knowledge of the fine differences among the prepositions that overlap in conceptual categories (e. g., *on*, *over*, *above*) is mostly confined to the isolated semantic representations of the prepositions. For example, when the learners are required to differentiate the three prepositions in the interview, the distinction is mostly made as follows: *On* gives prominence to "contiguity", *over* highlights "perpendicularity" and *above* puts stress on "noncontiguity". Little attention is paid to how categorization of objects bears on the use of the prepositions and how Chinese and English diverge in categorization of the objects. Therefore, their seemingly creative use of L2 is basically driven by L1-mediated spatial conceptualization. More evidence can be found in other degrees of equivalence. In Example (132), there are 14 participants from IG using the preposition *across*.

(132) There is a bend ________ the road.

According to participants' retrospective reports, the bend is considered as similar to the river winding across the road. Actually, what the preposition *across* designates is a spatial relationship involving two independent objects, but the bend in English is construed as part of the road rather than an object separated from the road. This means that the schematic landmark profiled by *across* does not correspond with the instance profiled by the noun *bend*, and therefore, the combination between the two structures is not permitted in English.

In a word, exposure to L2 spatial coding system promotes the modification of previously built conceptual structure with the internalization of some L2-specific conceptual features, but since the focus is on the semantic representations of prepositions rather than the object concept assigning the semantic values, the use of prepositions is still largely motivated by L1-specific categorization.

Secondly, the interaction between L2 proficiency and degrees of equivalence is also observed in LG. The statistical analysis reveals that the frequency of *in* for Equivalence IV is the lowest. Analysis of learner data shows that the two prepositions *from* and *through* are significantly preferred over the preposition *in* regardless of the prototypicality of the reference objects. This further confirms that LG is liable to establish a full equivalence between *cong* +*N* and *from*/*through* + *N*.

The above two findings about the interaction effect of L2 proficiency and degrees of equivalence indicate that the partial equivalence between English and Chinese causes much trouble to both LG and IG. For one thing, the overgeneralization of similarities between translation equivalents by LG tends to facilitate the occurrence of negative transfer. For another, IG's conservativeness in transferring prohibits the occurrence of positive transfer. Nemser and Slama-Cazacu (1970: 105) noted that the highest degree of difficulty seems to be found in the case of partial similarities. But a high frequent use of *in* by HG with these degrees of equivalence indicates the increase in L2 experience might help learners form a proper judgment of similarities between English and Chinese and result in the reduction of negative transfer caused by the partial cross-linguistic equivalence. Additionally, teachers' comprehensive cross-linguistic comparisons of spatial categorization are also greatly needed to facilitate the establishment of correct interlingual identity between translation equivalents.

To summarize, while there is some evidence of the changes of the effect of prototypicality in defining the elaborative distance, degrees of equivalence in the CONTAINER category are still found to play a more important role in motivating the use of *in*. Even the response of HG is affected by negative transfer in the case of lower degrees of equivalence. Therefore, the hypothesis about the developmental change of the effect of prototypicality with L2 proficiency is partially supported. Based on these findings, the analytic model for the formation of the construction [IN + N] by L2 learners might be modified (see Figure 6. 5) to reflect the overriding influence of degrees of equivalence on the use of *in* by L2 learners.

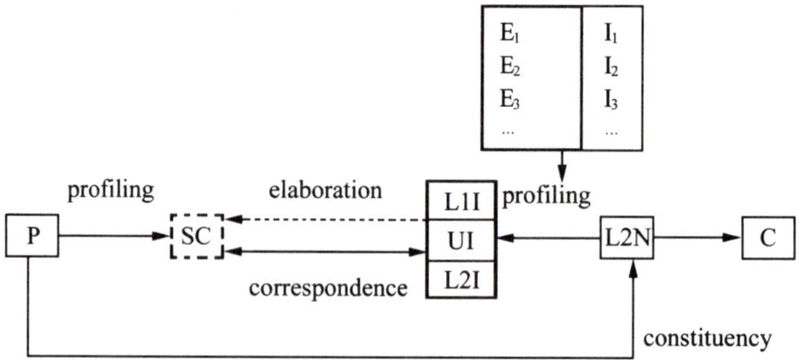

Figure 6.5 Modified Autonomy-dependency Analytic Model for the Formation of [IN+N] by L2 Learners

In this model, the box enclosing *En* is enlarged and boldfaced to highlight that degree of equivalence is more decisive in defining the elaborative distance. And the box enclosing *L1I* is also enlarged in order to emphasize L1-specific instance is more likely to be profiled. With the model, the conceptual mechanism of L1 transfer in the use of *in* by L2 learners is clearly revealed.

6.5 Summary

This chapter is intended to report and discuss the results of the study in hopes of uncovering the conceptual basis of L1 transfer in Chinese-speaking learners' use of the English spatial preposition *in*. Repeated measures ANOVA is run for statistical analysis of the quantitative data. The results are summarized as follows:

(1) Both prototypicality and degrees of equivalence have significant effects on participants' use of *in*.

(2) The variation in using *in* across degrees of equivalence exhibits a linear decrease, but the variation across the prototypical context does not.

(3) L2 proficiency has a significant main effect on participants' use of *in* in each prototypical context. Except Type V and VI containers, the use of *in* increases with the improvement of L2 proficiency. The effect of prototypicality changes significantly with the variation in L2 proficiency, but the linear rise in the use of *in* with increasing prototypicality is only observed in the responses of

HG.

(4) L2 proficiency has a significant main effect on participants' use of *in* in each typological context. Except Equivalence III, the use of *in* goes up as L2 proficiency increases. Besides, the variation in L2 proficiency also causes the effect of degrees of equivalence to change significantly.

On the basis of the results, the study explores the conceptual basis of the use of *in* by L2 learners and discusses the changes of the effects of prototypicality and degrees of equivalence with the variation in L2 proficiency. The major findings are as follows:

(1) Both prototypicality and degrees of equivalence are involved in defining the elaborative distance between the schematic container and the object concept profiled by the noun. This provides support for the model established in Chapter Three to account for the formation of the construction [IN + N] by L2 learners.

(2) Degrees of cross-linguistic equivalence in categorization override prototypicality in defining the elaborative distance. It might be reasonably assumed that degrees of equivalence constitute the conceptual mechanism of L1 transfer.

(3) More involvement of prototypicality in defining the elaborative distance with improving L2 proficiency causes a gradual reduction of negative conceptual transfer. But degrees of equivalence still play a decisive role in defining the elaborative distance. Therefore, the hypothesized change of the effect of prototypicality is partially supported.

(4) In the case of partial equivalence in construing containers, IG and LG are more likely to be affected by L1-based categorization without the establishment of a proper subjective similarity.

In the light of the above findings, a modified analytic model for the formation of [IN + N] by L2 learners is proposed, through which the conceptual impetus of L1 transfer in the use of *in* is revealed.

Chapter Seven Conclusion

7.1 Major Findings

On the basis of the theoretical framework established in Chapter Three, the researcher proposes an analytic model accounting for the formation of the composite spatial structure by L2 learners and hypothesizes that: (1) Use of English spatial prepositions by Chinese-speaking learners who have internalized and automatized L1-based category system would be prone to the influence of degree of equivalence in categorization between English and Chinese at the early stage of L2 learning; (2) As L2 proficiency increases there would be more involvement of L2-based category system, resulting in a developmental variation of conceptual transfer from L1; (3) Given sufficient L2 experience, the linkage between the form and L2-based category system would be automatized and a successful escape from L1-specific categorization would be achieved. To test the hypotheses, the researcher, by focusing on the spatial preposition *in*, carries out an empirical investigation of the effects of prototypicality and degrees of equivalence in the CONTAINER category on the use of *in* by Chinese-speaking English learners at different levels of L2 proficiency.

7.1.1 Findings of the Effect of Prototypicality

Following the formula S>T=V proposed by Langacker (1987: 371), prototypicality to a large extent defines how well the instances profiled by the nominal predicates elaborate the schematic container profiled by the preposition *in* and thereby determines the possibility of the integration between *in* and the nouns. To be precise, the more prototypical the reference object is, the more potential for the formation of the construction [IN+N] there is. According to connectionism (Ellis 2011, 2013; Wang 2001), frequency of L2 input is the function of the strength of links among the conceptual features defining the category of CONTAINER. This implies that prototypicality of reference objects might be an important cognitive factor motivating the access of *in* and its effect would be stronger with the increase of exposure to L2 input.

Based on the studies by Hottenroth (1993) and Cuyckens (1993), a classification of containers related to the different senses of the English spatial preposition *in* is established. It divides the instances of the CONTAINER category into seven types in terms of prototypicality with a geometrical-functional approach. The learners' use of *in* in each prototypical context is elicited by a preposition test and the evidence of L1 transfer is collected by a series of comparisons and a retrospective interview. The use of *in* with each type of containers is calculated and repeated measures ANOVA is performed for the statistical analysis of the quantitative data.

According to the statistical analysis, the major findings about the effect of prototypicality and its changes with L2 experience could be summarized as follows:

Firstly, the significant difference in the use of *in* across the seven prototypical contexts reveals that prototypicality has a significant effect on participants' use of *in*. This implies that the nominal predicates designating the containers of different prototypicality would have different potentials for motivating the use of *in*. However, the variation in the use of *in* across different prototypical contexts does not exhibit a linear decrease with declining prototypicality. Pairwise comparisons indicate that the effect of prototypicality works under the constraint of degrees of cross-linguistic equivalence in categorization. For a peripheral member, the high degree of cross-linguistic equivalence in categorization would strengthen its effect on the use of *in*, whereas for a relatively prototypical member, the difference in categorization would lengthen the elaborative distance between it and the schematic container. If the member is of both strong prototypicality and high degree of equivalence, it would be of the shortest distance. The above findings on the one hand verify the significant impact of prototypicality of reference objects on learners' access of *in* and demonstrate L2 learning is a process of restructuring the conceptual structure (Pavlenko 2009); on the other hand, they reveal that the effect of prototypicality seems to be constrained by how L2 and L1 converge in construing the objects as containers. This suggests that degrees of equivalence exert an overriding influence on the elaborative distance.

Secondly, the question of whether the effect of prototypicality changes with L2 experience is addressed in the following two aspects: the variation in the use of *in* for each prototypical context across the three proficiency groups and the variation across the seven prototypical contexts for each proficiency group. The results of the main effect of L2 proficiency show that except Type V and VI containers, the use of *in* goes up as L2 proficiency increases. Especially HG's use of *in* is considerably more frequent than that of the other two proficiency groups. This illustrates that the improvement of L2 proficiency strengthens the effect of prototypicality and causes a developmental variation in conceptual transfer. But concerning Types V and VI, there is a U-shaped variation in the use of *in*, which shows that for the two-dimensional containers, the improvement of L2 proficiency does not result in the increase in the effect of prototypicality. Analysis of leaner data reveals that the reasons accounting for the U-shaped variation are mainly summarized as follows: (1) Learning chunks by rote in the middle school does not promote the internalization of L2-based concepts; (2) Increase in L2 lexical knowledge encourages learners to choose prepositions which they assume would be more precise in verbalizing the geometrical features of the objects (e. g. *across the continent*), but because the focus is on the decontextualized senses of preposition in learning, they do not acquire the object concept elaborating the schematic landmark profiled by these prepositions and their creative use of prepositions is still driven by L1-based categorization.

The interaction effect of L2 proficiency and prototypicality shows that for HG, when the degrees of equivalence are similar to each other across the prototypical contexts, the use of *in* rises as prototypicality of containers increases. This implies that when degrees of equivalence are kept constant, prototypicality would play an important part in defining the elaborative distance. The more prototypical the container is, the shorter the distance is.

Then the use of *in* is conceptually dependent on prototypicality of containers. But as to the variation across all types of containers, there is no indication that the use of *in* declines linearly with the decreasing prototypicality. Therefore, it can be said that even HG has not yet established prototypicality-dominated pattern of categorization. This leads partial support to the assumption that the great increase in L2 exposure might promote the development of prototypicality-based categorization.

For LG, the interaction between L2 proficiency and prototypicality shows that the effect of prototypicality is weakened with the use of *in* with Type I containers dropping behind Types VI and VII. The misuse of the preposition *at* and the preposition *from/through* is mainly responsible for the reduction of *in*. As revealed in learner data, different from IG who seeks more verbal specification with the increase in vocabulary size, LG is more likely to choose a preposition that indicates nonspecific reference (e. g. *at*). In addition, because of inadequate L2 experience, the beginners are more ready to establish a full equivalence between the translation equivalents that are similar in form but partially equivalent in concepts.

To sum up, prototypicality of reference objects has a significant effect on the use of *in*, but the effect is constrained by degrees of cross-linguistic equivalence. And the effect of prototypicality is also observed to change with a gradual accumulation of L2 experience. Generally speaking, the increase in L2 experience would promote the internalization of L2 spatial concepts, but could not result in a native-like construal of the reference objects without the interference of L1-specific categorization. Therefore, the hypothesized developmental change of the effect of prototypicality is partially supported.

7.1.2 Findings of the Effect of the Degree of Cross-linguistic Equivalence

As an interlingual dimension of categorization, degrees of cross-linguistic equivalence are also hypothesized to be an important cognitive factor in defining the elaborative distance between the schematic container and the specifications of CONTAINER. In Chapter Two and Chapter Three, degrees of cross-linguistic equivalence are empirically and theoretically established as an important predictor for the occurrence of L1 transfer. Thus, an empirical study of the effect of degrees of cross-linguistic equivalence on learners' use of *in* would further illustrate how the production of the spatial prepositions is conceptually dependent on the construal of the nominal predicates and how the construal is influenced by L1-based categorization with different degrees of equivalence in categorization.

On the basis of analyzing data from the three corpora: BNC, CCLC and GCEPC, a continuum of cross-linguistic equivalence in the CONTAINER category between English and Chinese is established. The effect of degrees of cross-linguistic equivalence in categorization and its change with L2 experience are statistically analyzed via the repeated measures ANOVA.

Following the statistical reports, the major findings about the effect of degrees of equivalence and its change with the variation in L2 experience could be summarized as follows:

Firstly, degrees of cross-linguistic equivalence on the use of *in* have a significant effect on learners' preference for the preposition *in*. As the equivalence continuum moves from full, partial to zero, the use of *in* goes down linearly. For the last two degrees of equivalence where there tends to be zero overlap in categorizing containers between English and Chinese, the elaborative distance between the object concept and the schematic container is the longest. The analysis of learner data, L1 data and retrospective data shows that this is mainly attributed to the interference of L1-specific pattern of categorization. And conversely, in the case of full conceptual equivalence, *in* is used most frequently even though there are some reference objects that are classified as peripheral members of the CONTAINER category. Then when the equivalence moves from full to partial, there is a noticeable reduction in the use of *in*. Analysis of evidence of L1 transfer confirms a significant increase in the negative conceptual transfer. In addition, from Equivalence III, the use of *in* stays low. Wode (1978, cited in Larsen-Freeman & Long 2000: 96) noted only if L1 and L2 have structures meeting a crucial similarity measure will there be interference. Thus, Equivalence III where the category CONTAINER falls into more than one category in Chinese and CONTAINER is not a dominant pattern of categorization might be considered the crucial similarity measure that the L2 structures meet to trigger the interference of L1. The above findings demonstrate that the use of *in* by L2 learners is more dependent on degrees of equivalence in categorization. It is more decisive in defining the elaborative distance and constitutes the conceptual mechanism of L1 transfer.

Secondly, the results of the main effect of L2 proficiency for each degree of equivalence show that except Equivalence III, the use of *in* goes up in the linear manner with increasing L2 experience. Especially HG's use of *in* with each degree of equivalence is significantly more frequent than that of the other two groups. This implies that the improvement of L2 proficiency brings about a linear increase in the positive transfer caused by the interlingual similarities and a linear reduction in the negative transfer arising from the interlingual dissimilarities. Since subjective similarity is claimed to be the actual motivator for the occurrence of transfer (Jarvis & Pavlenko 2008; Kellerman 1995; Ringbom 2007), the finding indicates that with more L2-based spatial conceptual features being internalized, learners' judgment of the language distance is more and more convergent with the objective distance. However, it could also be seen that in the case of lower degrees of equivalence, HG also suffers much from negative transfer. This means that the increase of L2 experience could promote the development of L2-based categorization but could not lead to the dominance of prototypicality-based categorization and free learners from the influence of L1-based categorization completely.

In the case of Equivalence III, the use of *in* by IG does not rise but declines slightly. The interaction effect of L2 proficiency and degrees of equivalence further shows that IG's use of *in* with Equivalence III is less frequent than with Equivalence VI. In other words, the shorter language distance in Equivalence III does not inhibit the negative influence of L1-based categorization on IG's responses. One of the major reasons for the occurrence of negative conceptual transfer is that in the case of partial similarities, IG shows more conservativeness in transferring L1 knowledge which inhibits the positive transfer of L1.

The change of the effect of degrees of cross-linguistic equivalence with the L2 experience is also found in LG whose use of *in* with Equivalence IV reaches the lowest point. Analysis of learner data and evidence of L1 transfer shows that the strongest negative effect for the beginners is mainly caused by the assumed full equivalence between the translation equivalents: *cong* and *from*/*through*. This further confirms that the beginners are more ready to establish full equivalence between the translation equivalents that are formally similar to each other but partially convergent in the conceptual structure.

To recapitulate, though the increase in L2 proficiency could strengthen the effect of prototypicality, the use of *in* is still more conceptually dependent on degrees of cross-linguistic equivalence in categorization. Higher degrees of equivalence would facilitate the occurrence of positive transfer. As degrees of equivalence decline, there is an increase of negative transfer from L1-based categorization. Therefore, it might be reasonably assumed that degrees of cross-linguistic equivalence in construing containers constitute the conceptual mechanism of L1 transfer.

7.2 Implications of the Research

This research, though it is not exempt from the drawbacks, does have several important implications theoretically, methodologically, and pedagogically.

7.2.1 Theoretical Implications

The present research on the conceptual impetus of L1 transfer is driven by the newest developments in transfer studies, cognitive linguistics and bilingual mental research and it would in turn contribute to their sustainable developments with insightful findings.

Firstly, the findings of the constraint of degrees of cross-linguistic equivalence on the effect of prototypicality and the changes of the effects of the two factors with the variation in L2 experience provide more empirical evidence for the conceptual transfer hypothesis and deepen our understanding of the cognitive mechanism of L1 transfer. In particular, the research indicates that for the relational predicates which are conceptually dependent on the autonomous structures, the deep-rooted mechanism for the transfer tends to lie in the construal of the autonomous structures. This would motivate a conceptual approach to the studies of transfer in the acquisition of other relational predicates (e. g. verbs, adjectives or adverbs).

Secondly, for cognitive linguistics, the research is contributory in that it provides interlanguage evidence for Neo-Whorfianism, prototype theory and cognitive grammar and enhances the applicability of these hypotheses to the research on L2 acquisition. The verification of the significant effect of prototypicality-based categorization and the exploration of its changes with L2 experience well illustrate how L2 learning exerts its influence on the spatial thoughts and to what extent. This will promote the changes in the paradigm of the research on the relationship between language and thought, for example, focus might be shifted from the static description of the language particulars in conceptualization to the exploration of the dynamic changes in concepts with the increase of L2 proficiency. The results that participants' use of *in* varies along the continuum of prototypicality and the continuum of cross-linguistic equivalence in categorization confirm that the categorization is performed along the interlingual and intralingual dimensions, and the finding of the overriding influence of L1-based concepts further specifies that for L2 learners, their categorization is more subject to degrees of cross-linguistic equivalence. And finally with regard to Langacker's (1987) valence relation theory and the Analytic Model of Autonomy-dependency Alignment proposed by Niu (2011b) which have been widely used to account for the conceptual basis of the formation of a grammatical composite structure (Niu 2008a, 2008b, 2011a) but attracted little attention in the field of L2 acquisition, the confirmation of the effects of prototypicality of containers and degrees of equivalence in the CONTAINER category on the use of *in* provides cross-linguistic evidence for the claims about conceptual dependence of the relational predicates on the nominal predicates. In addition, on the basis of Niu's analytic model, an attempt is made to establish an analytic model explaining the generation of the construction [IN + N] by L2 learners. This enhances the explanatory power of Langacker's (1987) valence relation theory and Niu's Analytic Model (2011b) and promotes further application of cognitive grammar to L2 learning and teaching.

Thirdly, with regard to the implications for bilingual mental research, first of all, the demonstration of the involvement of the two systems of categorization in motivating the use of the English spatial preposition *in* lends empirical support to the interrelated nature of bilingual conceptual representation. In particular, the findings of the dominance of degrees of equivalence in affecting learners' use of *in* confirm the representational asymmetry between the translation equivalents claimed by Sense Model

(Finkbeiner 2002). In addition, the observation of the effect of prototypicality in HG offers evidence for the frequency effects in L2 learning argued by connectionist accounts of L2 learning (Ellis 2011, 2013; Wang 2001). Last but not least, the finding that the access of *in* is dependent on the conceptual representation of nouns will encourage researchers to think how to capture bilingual learners' processing of the relational predicates like *in*.

7.2.2 Methodological Implications

Concerning methodological implications, first of all, a brave attempt is made to take a corpus-based approach to the exploration of the cross-linguistic differences and similarities in construal of containers. Given translationese in parallel corpus which might distort the cross-linguistic differences and similarities in conceptualization (Granger 2010: 2), two comparable corpora are adopted as reference corpora: BNC and CCLC. The combination of the two types of corpora is significant in that it not only facilitates the establishment of a common platform of comparison in text types, semantics whereby the differences could be identified (Granger 2010: 2), but also helps in overcoming the problem of translationese and increasing the reliability of the comparative studies (Granger 2010: 5). Secondly, in the empirical research on the effects of prototypicality and degrees of equivalence on the use of *in*, four types of comparisons are made to confirm the presence of transfer effects. They are: (1) A comparison of learner data in a given context to discover the commonness in the use of prepositions among the participants; (2) A comparison of learner data across different contexts to identify the diversity in learner data; (3) A comparison between learner data and the corresponding L1 data to seek the correspondence between the two types of data; (4) A comparison between learner data and English native data to identify the difference in preferential choices of prepositions. With L2 acquisition being subject to the influence of multifarious factors, the first logical step is to disentangle L1 influence from other factors by collecting multiple sources of evidence for L1 transfer which will be cross-checked against each other to verify whether L1-related effects work or do not work in learners' use of a specific preposition.

7.2.3 Pedagogical Implications

It has long been recognized (Celce-Murcia & Larsen-Freeman 1999; Ma 2007; Tyler, Mueller & Ho 2011) that it is notoriously difficult for English learners to use English spatial prepositions in the native-like manner. The interference from cross-linguistic differences is one of the chief factors to blame. The introspective reports of some participants have shown that there are some problems with L2 vocabulary teaching and learning methods which not only facilitate the negative transfer of L1 but also inhibit the positive transfer. Therefore, in what follows several important implications from the research are presented.

Firstly, since object concepts are represented by the nouns following the prepositions, the research well demonstrates the influence of the linguistic context on the learners' choice of L2 forms. This strongly suggests that preposition teaching should not be confined to the presentation and instruction of the decontextualized senses of prepositions, but also be dedicated to directing learners' attention to the nouns collocating with the prepositions. As early as 1950s, Firth (1957, cited in Evert 2014: 2) underlined the importance of collocation by pointing out " knowing a word by the company it keeps". Teaching words in the collocational context will on the one hand help learners understand the conceptual basis of the senses of the spatial prepositions, and on the other hand, will raise learners' awareness of the importance of the collocation in vocabulary learning on the whole. However, teaching collocations does not mean requiring learners to learn the collocations as formulas by rote. As shown in the study, learning by rote might promote native-like use of the prepositions without the interference from L1 at the beginning, but fail to result in the internalization of the concepts represented by the grammatical construction.

Secondly, as revealed in the research, conceptual transfer involves both positive transfer and negative transfer. Since the transfer is actually motivated by the learners' subjective similarity (Kellerman 1995; Jarvis & Pavlenko 2008), it is indispensible for the teachers to guide learners to form a proper judgment of the language distance with explicit comparisons of patterns of spatial categorization between English and Chinese. Especially for the typological context where English and Chinese partially overlap in categorization, the teachers are expected to direct learners to identify where they converge and where they diverge. This will not only facilitate the occurrence of the positive effect of L1, but also inhibit the negative transfer triggered by the overgeneralization of similarities. The detailed descriptions of different degrees of equivalence in categorization between English and Chinese would promise a practical guidance for the teachers.

Thirdly, the increase in L2 experience is found to enable some learners to produce the prepositions with more complex conceptual representations, like *across*, but their production is basically driven by the object concept profiled by the Chinese equivalent, like *across a continent*. An important implication is that the increase in vocabulary size does not necessarily result in an establishment of the linkage between the form and L2-mediated concepts. In current L2 vocabulary learning, development of vocabulary breadth is always given much priority to the exclusion of whether learners have internalized the conceptual representations of the words. This gives birth to many grammatically correct but semantically anomalous L2 expressions. Therefore, in English teaching teachers are expected to attach equal importance to the development of vocabulary depth. By means of explicit instruction, provision of English explanations or presentation of conceptual schemas to visualize the differences between the words and their translation equivalents, teachers inform learners of the conceptual basis underlying the use of a specific L2 word and promote the establishment of the direct links between concepts and L2 forms. Besides, the finding of the induced errors also issues a call for the improvement of teachers' knowledge of English. The prototypicality-based classification of the instances of CONTAINER delineated by the present research could be included in the textbooks or reference books to increase both teachers' and learners' conceptual knowledge of L2 spatial coding system.

Fourthly, the finding of the interaction between L2 proficiency and prototypicality and degrees of equivalence shows that the increase in exposure to L2 would motivate the internalization of L2-specific concepts, and cause a reduction in negative transfer. However, it is also observed that even HG is greatly affected by the interference of the L1-specific categorization. This implies that learning to think and speak in English involves much more than the increase in L2 exposure.

Therefore, what teachers are concerned about is not only how much the exposure learners need but also what type of exposure they need.

7.3 Limitations of the Research

Although the research provides important implications as mentioned above, it is also found problematic in the measurement of L2 proficiency, the design of the test paper and the ignorance of other contextual factors influencing the use of the preposition *in*.

As noted in Chapter Four, following the trend in conceptual transfer research, L2 proficiency is defined in terms of the length of exposure to L2. But in a cross-sectional research design, there tends to be a neglect of the individual differences which might cause the learners with more years of English learning to be not always more proficient than the learners with fewer years, especially in the classroom-based foreign language learning setting. Thus, given sufficient time, longitudinal research is recommended.

Secondly, concerning the preposition test, the number of the items across the sets is not the same. For example, for the set testing the effect of Type VII containers, there are only two items because of the low frequency of the integration between the preposition *in* and the nouns denoting the one-dimensional objects. And for the set testing the effect of Equivalence V and Equivalence VI, the number of the items is nine and four respectively. One important reason for the unequalness is that few instances for some typological contexts are found in GCEPC. Such an unequal distribution might have a bearing on the research results.

Thirdly, although construal of reference objects is generally assumed to be more important in assigning the senses of prepositions and has been empirically demonstrated in the present research, it is not the sole cognitive factor involved. Since the located object is also a necessary participant in a given spatial event, categorization of located objects should also be examined. Besides, the conceptual structure of verbs should also arouse some concern of the researcher in future research, especially if the research is concerned with the conceptual transfer in the acquisition of dynamic prepositions, like *over*, *across* or *through*.

7.4 Suggestions for Future Research

The research is one of the first empirical attempts at the exploration of the conceptual transfer from the perspective of categorization of objects. Although it gives rise to more in-depth understandings of conceptual transfer, the limitations and the developmental trends in transfer research reveal that there are still some issues worthy of further investigation.

First of all, future research should be dedicated to establishing a general explanatory framework for the conceptual transfer occurring in the domain of space. For this purpose, what is needed firstly is expanding the scope of the research on conceptual transfer by adding new language items or independent variables for investigation. Actually, in the present study, it has been found that some prepositions like *across* or *by* also cause much trouble to the learners and there also seems to be a systematic variation in the use of those prepositions under the constraint of the L1-based categorization. Besides reference objects, of the contextual constraints on the semantic assignment of the spatial prepositions enumerated by Zhang (2013: 13), the construal of the located objects and the construal of the motion events are also two other important factors influencing the use of spatial prepositions and therefore, they also constitute new promising areas for exploration. One more area calling for investigation is the conceptual transfer in the comprehension of spatial prepositions. The cross-cultural variety in categorization might also interfere with native-like understanding of the spatial relations. For example,

(133) There is a bridge across the river.

If learners fail to classify the reference object "river" as a path that is contiguous to the bridge, the bridge will not be construed as a floating bridge and the preposition *across* will be considered as synonymous with the preposition *over*.

Secondly, more longitudinal and microgenetic studies are needed to get more reliable and valid data about the developmental variation in conceptual transfer in relation to the changes in L2 experience. To the knowledge of the researcher, the conceptual transfer research is still predominated by the cross-sectional design. With the employment of different measurements of L2 proficiency and the intervention of individual differences, the conclusions about the developmental variation of transfer from the cross-sectional studies are not consistent, or even contradictory with one another. However, longitudinal and microgenetic studies are more advantageous in providing developmental data by keeping track of the developmental changes of the same individuals over a long period of time. One major difference between the two research approaches is that the former takes a longer time, but is less demanding on the density of the examination, and the latter runs in the opposite direction (Wen 2004). Thus the two approaches can be complementary to each other to help the researchers track the changes of transfer more scientifically.

Thirdly, more importance should also be attached to conceptual transfer in the acquisition of metaphoric senses of English prepositions. There has been an increasing recognition that metaphorical competence is one of the criteria for evaluating whether L2 learners have reached native-level fluency (Danesi 1995: 5; Liu & Shi 2013). In addition, there is a wider cross-linguistic difference in mapping the spatial coding system metaphorically onto the abstract domain of experience (Boers & Demecheleer 1998). In the light of GCEPC, it can be found that many prepositional structures in their metaphorical use correspond with verbal or adverbial structures in Chinese. For instance,

(134) They walked <u>in a stooped posture</u>.
他们<u>弯着腰</u>走路。

(135) He passed some time <u>in tortures of suspense</u>.
他<u>提心吊胆地</u>忙了十来分钟。(GCEPC)

Therefore, it is of great necessity to make comparative studies on the categorization of the abstract spatial domain and to empirically test the cross-linguistic effects in developing native-like metaphorical competence.

Finally, with increasing interest in the transfer occurring in the third language learning, the conceptual transfer in the acquisition of L3 spatial prepositions is also an issue awaiting examination. This will not only be contributory to revealing the conceptual mechanism of transfer in multi-language learning, but also will provide more evidence for the influence of language on cognition.

References

Aijmer, K. & Altenberg, B. (1996). Introduction. In K. Aijmer, B. Altenberg & M. Johansson (eds.), *Languages in Contact: Papers from a Symposium on Text-based Cross-linguistic Studies* (pp. 11-16). Lund: Lund University Press.

Alderson, J. C., Clapham, C. & Wall, D. (2000). *Language Test Construction and Evaluation*. Beijing: Foreign Language Teaching and Research Press.

Andersen, R. (1983). Transfer to somewhere. In S. Gass & L. Selinker (eds.), *Language Transfer in Language Learning* (pp. 177-201). Rowley, MA: Newbury House.

Ard, J. & Homburg, T. (1992). Verification of language transfer. In S. Gass & L. Selinker (eds.), *Language Transfer in Language Learning* (pp. 47-70). Amsterdam/Philadelphia: John Benjamins Publishing Company.

Aurnague, M., Hickmann, M. & Vieu, L. (2007). Searching for the categorization of spatial entities in language and cognition. In M. Aurnague, M. Hickmann & L. Vieu (eds.), *The Categorization of Spatial Entities in Language and Cognition* (pp. 1-32). Amsterdam/Philadelphia: John Benjamins Publishing Company.

Becker, A. & Carroll, M. (1997). *The Acquisition of Spatial Relations in a Second Language*. Amsterdam/Philadelphia: John Benjamins Publishing Company.

Berlin, B. & Kay, P. (1969). *Basic Color Terms: Their Universality and Evolution*. Berkeley: University of California Press.

Bhattacharya, H. (2008). Interpretive research. In L. Given (ed.), *The SAGE Encyclopedia of Qualitative Research Methods* (pp. 465-468).

Thousand Oaks, CA: SAGE Publications, Inc.

BNC Website: http: //corpus. byu. edu/bnc.

Boers, F. & Demecheleer, M. (1998). A cognitive semantic app roach to teaching prepositions. *English Language Teaching Journal*, 52 (3), 197-204.

Bohnacker, U. & Rosen, C. (2008). The clause-initial position in L2 German declaratives: Transfer of information structure. *Studies in Second Language Acquisition*, 30(4), 511-538.

Boroditsky, L. (2001). Does language shape thought? Mandarin and English speakers' conceptions of time. *Cognitive Psychology*, 43(1), 1-22.

Bowerman, M. (1996a). Learning how to structure space for language: A cross-linguistic perspective. In P. Bloom, M. Peterson, L. Nadel & M. Garrett (eds.), *Language and Space* (pp: 385-436). Cambridge, MA: MIT Press.

Bowerman, M. (1996b). The origins of children's spatial semantic categories: Cognitive versus linguistic determinants. In J. Gumperz & S. Levinson (eds.), *Rethinking Linguistic Relativity* (pp. 145-176). Cambridge, UK: Cambridge University Press.

Bowerman, M. (2007). Containment, support, and beyond: Constructing topological spatial categories in first language acquisition. In M. Aurnague, M. Hickmann & L. Vieu (eds.), *The Categorization of Spatial Entities in Language and Cognition* (pp. 177-203). Amsterdam/Philadelphia: John Benjamins Publishing Company.

Bowerman, M. & Choi, S. (2003). Space under construction: Language-specific spatial categorization in first language acquisition. In D. Gentner & S. Goldin-Meadow (eds.), *Language in Mind: Advances in the Study of Language and Thought* (pp. 387-427). Cambridge, MA: MIT Press.

CCLC Website: http: //ccl. pku. edu. cn: 8080/ccl_corpus/index. jsp? dir=xiandai.

Celce-Murcia, M. & Larsen-Freeman, D. (1999). *The Grammar Book: An ESL/EFL Teacher's Course* (Second Edition). Boston, MA: Heinle & Heinle.

Chandler, D. (2004). *Semiotics: The Basics* (Second Edition). New York: Routledge.

Choi, S. (2006). Influence of language-specific input on spatial cognition:

Categories of containment. *First Language*, 26(2), 207-232.

Churchill, E. & DuFon, M. A. (2006). Evolving threads in study abroad research. In M. A. DuFon & E. Churchill (eds.), *Language Learners in Study Abroad Contexts* (pp. 1-27). Clevedon, UK: Multilingual Matters.

Clarke, A. M., Losoff, A., McCracken, D. M. & Still, J. (1981). Gender perception in Arabic and English. *Language Learning*, 31(1), 159-169.

Cook, V., Bassetti, B., Kasai, C., Sasaki, M. & Takahashi, J. A. (2006). Do bilinguals have different concepts? The case of shape and material in Japanese L2 users of English. *International Journal of Bilingualism*, 10(2), 137-152.

Correa-Beningfield, M. R. (1985). *Prototype and Language Transfer: The Acquisition by Native Speakers of Spanish of Four Prepositions of Location*. Doctoral dissertation, Teachers' College of Columbia University, New York.

Coventry, K. & Garrod, S. (2004). *Saying, Seeing and Acting: The Psychological Semantics of Spatial Prepositions*. Hove: Psychology Press.

Cruse, D. A. (1990). Prototype theory and lexical semantics. In S. L. Tsohatzidis (ed.), *Meaning and Prototypes* (pp. 382-402). London: Routledge.

Cuyckens, H. (1993). The Dutch spatial preposition *in*: A cognitive-semantic analysis. In C. Zelinsky-Wibbelt (ed.), *The Semantics of Prepositions: From Mental Processing to Natural Language Processing* (pp. 27-71). Berlin/New York: Mouton de Gruyter.

Daller, M. H., Daller, J. T. & Furman, R. (2011). Transfer of conceptualization patterns in bilinguals: The construal of motion events in Turkish and German. *Bilingualism: Language and Cognition*, 14(1), 95-119.

Danesi, M. (1995). Learning and teaching languages: The role of conceptual fluency. *International Journal of Applied Linguistics*, 5(1), 3-20.

de Bot, K. (1992). A bilingual production model: Levelt's 'speaking' model adapted. *Applied Linguistics*, 13(1), 1-24.

de Groot, A. M. B. (1992). Bilingual lexical representation: A closer look at conceptual representations. In R. Frost & L. Katz (eds.), *Orthography Phonology, Morphology, and Meaning* (pp. 389-412).

Amsterdam: Elsevier.

Delija, S. & Koruti, O. (2013). Challenges in teaching prepositions in a language classroom. *Journal of Education and Practice*, 4(13), 124-130.

Dewaele J.-M. & Véronique, D. (2001). Gender assignment and gender agreement in advanced French interlanguage: A cross-sectional study. *Bilingualism: Language and Cognition*, 4(3), 275-297.

Ellis, N. C. (2011). Frequency-based accounts of SLA. In S. Gass & A. Mackey (eds.), *Handbook of Second Language Acquisition* (pp. 193-210). London: Routledge/Taylor Francis.

Ellis, N. C. (2013). Frequency-based grammar and the acquisition of tense-aspect in L2 learning. In R. Salaberry & L. Comajoan (eds.), *Research Design and Methodology in Studies on Second Language Tense and Aspect* (pp. 89-118). Berlin: Mouton de Gruyter.

Ellis, N. C. & Schmidt, R. (1997). Morphology and longer distance dependencies. *Studies in Second Language Acquisition*, 19, 145-171.

Ellis, R. (1999). *Understanding Second Language Acquisition*. Shanghai: Shanghai Foreign Language Education Press.

Evert, S. Corpora and collocations. http://www.stefan-evert.de/PUB/Evert2007 SK_extended_manuscript (accessed 07/08/2014).

Feist, M. I. & Gentner, D. (2012). Multiple influences on the use of English spatial prepositions: The case of *in* and *on*. In C. Boonthum-Denecke, P. M. McCarthy & T. Lamkin (eds.), *Cross-disciplinary Advances in Applied Natural Language Processing: Issues and Approaches* (pp. 305-323). Hershey, PA: IGI Global.

Finkbeiner, M. (2002). *Bilingual Lexical Memory: Towards a Psycholinguistic Model of Adult L2 Lexical Acquisition, Representation, and Processing*. Unpublished doctoral dissertation, University of Arizona, Arizona.

Finkbeiner, M. Acquisition of L2 spatial prepositions: New words for old concepts? http://slat.arizona.edu/sites/slat/files/page/awp6finkbeiner (accessed 05/6/2013).

Finton, J. D. (2002). *Cognitive Economy and the Role of Representation in On-line Learning*. Unpublished doctoral dissertation, University of Wisconsin-Madison, Madison, Wisconsin.

Garrod, S., Ferrier, G. & Campbell, S. (1999). *In* and *on*: Investigating the functional geometry of spatial prepositions. *Cognition*, 72(2), 167-189.

Gass, S. & Selinker, L. (2001). *Second Language Acquisition: An Introductory Course*. Mahwah, NJ: Lawrence Erlbaum.

Gellerstam, M. (1996). Translations as a source for cross-linguistic studies. In K. Aijmer, B. Altenberg & M. Johansson (eds.), *Language in Contrast: Papers from a Symposium on Text-based Cross-linguistic Studies* (pp. 53-62). Lund: Lund University Press.

Gentner, D. & Bowerman, M. (2009). Why some spatial semantic categories are harder to learn than others: The typological prevalence hypothesis. In J. Guo, E. Lieven, N. Budwig, S. Ervin-Tripp, K. Nakamura & S. Ozcaliskan (eds.), *Cross-linguistic Approaches to the Psychology of Language: Research in the Tradition of Dan Isaac Slobin* (pp. 465-480). New York: Psychology Press.

Graham, R. & Belnap, K. (1986). The acquisition of lexical boundaries in English by native speakers of Spanish. *International Review of Applied Linguistics in Language Teaching*, 24(4), 275-286.

Granger, S. (2010). Comparable and translation corpora in cross-linguistic research: Design, analysis and applications. *Journal of Shanghai Jiaotong University*, 2: 14-21.

Haberlandt, K. (1994). *Cognitive Psychology*. Massachusetts: Allyn & Bacon.

Harper, D. Online Etymology Dictionary. http: //www. Etymonline (accessed 23/08/2014).

Herskovits, A. (1986). *Language and Spatial Cognition: An Interdisciplinary Study of the Prepositions in English*. Cambridge: Cambridge University Press.

Hohenstein, J., Eisenberg, A. & Naigles, L. (2006). Is he floating across or crossing afloat? Cross-influence of L1 and L2 in Spanish-English bilingual adults. *Bilingualism: Language and Cognition*, 9(3), 249-261.

Holmes, V. & Dejean de la Batie, B. (1999). Assignment of grammatical gender by native speakers and foreign learners of French. *Applied Psycholinguistics*, 20(4), 479-506.

Hottenroth, P.-M. (1993). Prepositions and object concepts: A contribution to cognitive semantics. In C. Zelinsky-Wibbelt (ed.), *The Semantics of Prepositions: From Mental Processing to Natural Language Processing* (pp. 179-219). Berlin/New York: Mouton de Gruyter.

Hulstijn, J. H. (2002). Towards a unified account of the representation, processing and acquisition of second language knowledge. *Second Language Research*, 18(3), 193-223.

Ijaz, H. (1986). Linguistic and cognitive determinants of lexical acquisition in a second language. *Language Learning*, 36(4), 401-451.

Jackendoff, R. (1983). *Semantics and Cognition*. Cambridge, MA: MIT Press.

Jackendoff, R. (1990). *Semantic Structures*. Cambridge, MA: MIT Press.

Jarvis, S. (2007). Theoretical and methodological issues in the investigation of conceptual transfer. *Vigo International Journal of Applied Linguistics*, 4, 43-71.

Jarvis, S. (2010). Comparison-based and detection-based approaches to transfer research. In L. Roberts, M. Howard, M. Laoire & D. Singleton (eds.), *EUROSLA Yearbook 10* (pp. 169-192). Amsterdam/Philadelphia: John Benjamins Publishing Company.

Jarvis, S. (2011). Conceptual transfer: Cross-linguistic effects in categorization and construal. *Bilingualism: Language and Cognition*, 14(1), 1-8.

Jarvis, S. & Odlin, T. (2000). Morphological type, spatial reference, and language transfer. *Studies in Second Language Acquisition*, 22(4), 535-556.

Jarvis, S. & Pavlenko, A. (2008). *Crosslinguistic Influence in Language and Cognition*. New York: Routledge.

Kay, P. & McDaniel, C. (1978). The linguistic significance of the meanings of basic color terms. *Language*, 54(3), 610-646.

Kellerman, E. (1979). Transfer and non-transfer: Where are we now? *Studies in Second Language Acquisition*, 2(1), 37 57.

Kellerman, E. (1995). Cross-linguistic influence: Transfer to nowhere? *Annual Review of Applied Linguistics*, 15, 125-150.

Kelly, B. F. (2002). 'Well you can't put your swimsuit on top of your pants!': Child-mother uses of *in* and *on*. In E. V. Clark (ed.), *Proceedings of the 31st Stanford Child Language Research Forum* (pp. 10-21). Standford: CSLI.

Khampang, P. (1974). Thai difficulties in using English prepositions. *Language Learning*, 24(2), 215-222.

Koosha, M. & Jafarpour, A. (2006). Data-driven learning and teaching collocation of prepositions: The case of Iranian EFL adult learners. *Asian EFL Journal*, 8(8), 64-82.

Kroll, J. & Stewart, E. (1994). Category interference in translation and picture naming: Evidence for asymmetric connections between bilingual memory representations. *Journal of Memory and Language*, 33(2), 149-174.

Kroll, J. & Tokowicz, N. (2005). Models of bilingual representation and processing: Looking back and to the future. In J. F. Kroll & A. M. B. de Groot (eds.), *Handbook of Bilingualism: Psycholinguistic Approaches* (pp. 531-553). New York: Oxford University Press.

Labov, W. (1973). The boundaries of words and their meanings. In C.-J. Bailey & R. Shuy (eds.), *New Ways of Analyzing Variation in English* (pp: 340-373). Washington, D. C. : Georgetown University Press.

Lakoff, G. (1987). *Women, Fire, and Dangerous Things: What Categories Reveal about the Mind*. Chicago: The University of Chicago Press.

Landu, S. & Everitt, A. (2004). *Handbook of Statistical Analyses Using SPSS*. Boca Raton: Chapman & Hall/CRC.

Landau, B. & Jackendoff, R. (1993). "What" and "where" in spatial language and spatial cognition. *Behavioral and Brain Sciences*, 16(2), 217-265.

Langacker, R. (1987). *Foundations of Cognitive Grammar. Vol. I.* Stanford, CA: Stanford University Press.

Langacker, R. (2002). *The Cognitive Basis of Grammar* (Second Edition). Berlin: Mouton de Gruyter.

Langacker, R. (2008). *Cognitive Grammar: A Basic Introduction.* Oxford: Oxford University Press.

Larsen-Freeman, D. & Long, H. M. (2000). *An Introduction to Second Language Acquisition Research*. Beijing: Foreign Language Teaching and Research Press.

Laufer, B. (2010). Lexical threshold revisited: Lexical text coverage, learners' vocabulary size and reading comprehension. *Reading in a Foreign Language*, 22(1), 15-30.

Levinson, S. (2003). *Space in Language and Cognition: Explorations in Cognitive Diversity*. Cambridge: Cambridge University Press.

Li, P. (2006). Modeling language acquisition and representation: Connectionist networks. In P. Li, E. Bates, L. H. Tan & O. J. L. Tzeng (eds.), *Handbook of East Asian Psycholinguistics Vol. I: Chinese* (pp. 320-329). Cambridge: Cambridge University Press.

Lightbown, P. M. (1985). Great expectations: Second language acquisition research and classroom teaching. *Applied Linguistics*, 6 (2), 173-189.

Lightbown, P. M. (2000). Anniversary article: Classroom and SLA and second language teaching. *Applied Linguistics*, 21(4), 431-462.

Lightbown, P. M. & Spada, N. (1999). *How Languages are Learned*. Oxford: Oxford University Press.

Lindstromberg, S. (1997). *English Prepositions Explained*. Amsterdam/Philadelphia: John Benjamins Publishing Company.

Lucy, J. (1997). Linguistic relativity. *Annual Review of Anthropology*, 26(1), 291-312.

Ma, S. (2005). *The Acquisition of English Spatial Prepositional Semantics by Chinese EFL Learners*. Doctoral dissertation. Guangdong University of Foreign Studies, Guangzhou.

MacWhinney, B. (2007). The competition model: The input, the context, and the brain. In P. Robinson (ed.), *Cognition and Second Language Instruction* (pp. 69-90). Beijing: World Publishing Corporation.

Malt, B. C. & Sloman, S. (2003). Linguistic diversity and object naming by non-native speakers of English. *Bilingualism: Language and Cognition*, 6(1), 47-67.

Malt, B. C., Sloman, S. & Gennari, S. (2003). Universality and language specificity in object naming. *Journal of Memory and Language*, 49(1), 20-42.

Malt, B. C., Sloman, S., Gennari, S., Shi, M. & Wang, Y. (1999). Knowing versus naming: Similarity and the linguistic categorization of artifacts. *Journal of Memory and Language*, 40(2), 230-262.

McLaughlin, B. (1990). Restructuring. *Applied Linguistics*, 11(2), 113-128.

Mougeon, R. M. Canale, M. M. & Carroll, S. (1979). Acquisition of English prepositions by monolingual and bilingual (French/English) Ontarian students. In F. R. Eckman & A. J. Hastings (eds.), *Studies in First and Second Language Acquisition* (pp. 194-225). Rowley, MA: Newbury House.

Nemser, W. & Slama-Cazacu, T. (1970). A contribution to contrastive linguistics (A psychological approach: Contact analysis). *Revue Roumaine de Linguistique*, 15(2), 101-128.

Odlin, T. (1989). *Language Transfer: Cross-linguistic Influence in Language Learning*. Shanghai: Shanghai Foreign Language Education Press.

Odlin, T. (2005). Cross-linguistic influence and conceptual transfer: What are the concepts? *Annual Review of Applied Linguistics*, 25, 3-25.

Odlin, T. (2008). Conceptual transfer and meaning extensions. In P. Robinson & N. C. Ellis (eds.), *Handbook of Cognitive Linguistics and Second Language Acquisition* (pp. 306-340). New York/London: Routledge.

Oller, J. W. Jr. & Inal, N. (1971). A cloze test of English prepositions. *TESOL Quarterly*, 5(4), 315-326.

Online etymology dictionary website: www. etymonline. com.

Paribakht, T. S. (2005). The influence of first language lexicalization on second language lexical inferencing: A study of Farsi-speaking learners of English as a foreign language. *Language Learning*, 55(4), 701-748.

Pavesi, M. (1987). Lexical simplification in spatial prepositions. *ERIC*, 19(1), 97-107.

Pavlenko, A. (2002). Conceptual change in bilingual memory: A Neo-Whorfian approach. In F. Fabbro (ed.), *Advances in the Neurolinguistics of Bilingualism: Essays in Honor of Michel Paradis* (pp. 71-94). Udine: Udine University Press.

Pavlenko, A. (2009). Conceptual representation in the bilingual lexicon and second language vocabulary learning. In A. Pavlenko (ed.), *The Bilingual Mental Lexicon: Interdisciplinary Approaches to Lexical Transfer* (pp. 125-160). Clevedon, UK: Multilingual Matters.

Pavlenko, A. & Driagina, V. (2007). Russian emotion vocabulary in

American learners' narratives. *Modern Language Journal*, 91(2), 213-234.

Pavlenko, A. & Malt, B. C. (2011). Kitchen Russian: Cross-linguistic differences and first-language object naming by Russian-English bilinguals. *Bilingualism: Language and Cognition*, 14(1), 19-45.

Potter, C. M., So, K.-F., von Eckhardt, B. & Feldman, L. B. (1984). Lexical and conceptual representation in beginning and proficient bilinguals. *Journal of Verbal Learning and Verbal Behavior*, 23(1), 23-38.

Ringbom, H. (1978). The influence of the mother tongue on the translation of lexical items. *Interlanguage Studies Bulletin*, 3(1), 80-101.

Ringbom, H. (1986). Crosslinguistic influence and the foreign language learning process. In E. Kellerman & M. Sharwood Smith (eds.), *Crosslinguistic Influence in Second Language Acquisition* (pp. 150-162). Oxford: Pergamon Institute of English.

Ringbom, H. (2006). The importance of different types of similarity in transfer studies. In J. Arabski (ed.), *Cross-linguistic Influences in the Second Language Lexicon* (pp. 36-45). Clevedon, UK: Multilingual Matters.

Ringbom, H. (2007). *Cross-linguistic Similarity in Foreign Language Learning: Comprehension, Learning and Production*. Clevedon, UK: Multilingual Matters.

Rosch, E. (1973). On the internal structure of perceptual and semantic categories. In T. E. Moore (ed.), *Cognitive Development and the Acquisition of Language* (pp: 111-144). New York/San Francisco/London: Academic Press.

Rosch, E. (1975). Cognitive representations of semantic categories. *Journal of Experimental Psychology: General*, 104, 193-233.

Rosch, E. (1978). Principles of categorization. In E. Rosch & B. B. Lloyd (eds), *Cognition and Categorization* (pp. 27-48). Hillsdale, NJ: Lawrence Erlbaum.

Rosch, E. & Lloyd, B. B. (eds.). (1978). *Cognition and Categorization*. Hillsdale, NJ: Lawrence Erlbaum.

Rosch, E. & Mervis, C. B. (1975). Family resemblances: Studies in the internal structure of categories. *Cognitive Psychology*, 7(4), 573-605.

Rosch, E., Mervis, B., Gray, W. D., Johnson, D. M. & Bayes-Braem, P. (1976). Basic objects in natural categories. *Cognitive Psychology*,

8(3), 382-439.

Schumann, J. (1986). Locative and directional expressions in basilang speech. *Language Learning*, 36(3), 277-294.

Selinker, L. (1972). Interlanguage. *International Review of Applied Linguistics*, 10(3), 209-231.

Slobin, D. (1996). From "thought and language" to "thinking for speaking". In J. Gumperz & S. Levinson (eds.), *Rethinking Linguistic Relativity* (pp. 70-96). Cambridge, UK: Cambridge University Press.

Slobin, D. (2000). Verbalized events: A dynamic approach to linguistic relativity and determinism. In S. Niemeier & R. Dirven (eds.), *Evidence for Linguistic Relativity* (pp. 107-138). Berlin: Mouton de Gruyter.

Smolensky, P., Legendre, G. & Miyata, Y. (1992). Principles for an integrated connectionist/symbolic theory of higher cognition. *Technical Report CU-CS-600-92*. Boulder: Computer Science Department and Institute of Cognitive Science, University of Colorado at Boulder.

Sperber, D. & Wilson, D. (2001). *Relevance: Communication and Cognition*. Beijing: Foreign Language Education and Research Press.

Talmy, L. (1983). How language structures space. In H. L. Pick & L. P. Acredolo (eds.), *Spatial Orientation: Theory, Research, and Application* (pp. 225-282). New York/London: Plenum Press.

Talmy, L. (1991). Path to realization: A typology of event conflation. In L. A. Sutton, C. Johnson & R. Shields (eds.), *Proceedings of the Seventeenth Annual Meeting of the Berkeley Linguistics Society* (pp. 480-519). Berkeley, CA: Berkeley Linguistics Society.

Talmy, L. (2000). *Toward a Cognitive Semantics Vol. I: Concept Structuring Systems*. Cambridge, MA: MIT Press.

Taylor, J. (2001). *Linguistic Categorization: Prototypes in Linguistic Theory* (Second Edition). Oxford: Clarendon Press.

Taylor, J. (2002). *Cognitive Grammar*. Oxford: Oxford University Press.

Thomas, M. (1994). Assessment of L2 proficiency in second language acquisition research. *Language Learning*, 44(2), 307-336.

Tokowicz, N. & MacWhinney, B. (2005). Implicit and explicit measures of sensitivity to violations in second language grammar. *Studies in Second*

Language Acquisition, 27(2), 173-204.

Trofimovich, P., Gatbonton, E. & Segalowitz, N. (2007). A dynamic look at L2 phonological learning: Seeking processing explanations for implicational phenomena. *Studies in Second Language Acquisition*, 29(3), 407-448.

Tyler, A. & Evans, V. (2003). *The Semantics of English Prepositions: Spatial Scenes, Cognition and the Experiential Basis of Meaning*. New York/Cambridge: Cambridge University Press.

Tyler, A., Mueller, C. & Ho, V. (2011). Applying cognitive linguistics to learning the semantics of English *to*, *for* and *at*: An experimental investigation. *VIAL*, 8, 181-205.

Ungerer, F. & Schmid, H. J. (2001). *An Introduction to Cognitive Linguistics*. Beijing: Foreign Language Teaching and Research Press.

Vandeloise, C. (1994). Methodology and analyses of the preposition *in*. *Cognitive Linguistics*, 5(2), 157-184.

Vandeloise, C. (2005). Family resemblances and the structure of spatial relationships. *CORELA*, 3(2), 1-20.

Vandeloise, C. (2007). A taxonomy of basic natural entities. In M. Aurnague, M. Hickmann & L. Vieu (eds.), *The Categorization of Spatial Entities in Language and Cognition* (pp. 35-52). Amsterdam/Philadelphia: John Benjamins Publishing Company.

Wei, H. (2007). A study on the acquisition of L2 spatial prepositions by Chinese-speaking beginners of English: A case study of *in* and *on*. Unpublished master's thesis. Northwest Normal University, Lanzhou.

Wen, Q. (2004). *Applied Linguistics Research Methods and Thesis Writing*. Beijing: Foreign Language Teaching and Research Press.

Xiao, R. (2009). Theory-driven corpus research: Using corpora to inform aspect theory. In A. Ludeling & M. Kyto (eds.), *Corpus Linguistics: An International Handbook* (pp. 987-1008). Berlin: Mouton de Gruyter.

Yoon, K. (1993). Challenging prototype descriptions: Perception of noun countability and indefinite vs. zero article use. *International Review of Applied Linguistics*, 31(4), 269-289.

Young-Davy, B. (2000). *A Cognitive Semantic Approach to Acquisition of English Prepositions*. Doctoral dissertation, University of Oregon,

Eugene.

Zelinsky-Wibbelt, C. (1993). Introduction. In C. Zelinsky-Wibbelt (ed.), *The Semantics of Prepositions: From Mental Processing to Natural Language Processing* (pp. 1-24). Berlin/New York: Mouton de Gruyter.

蔡金亭:《在二语习得研究中确定母语迁移的方法》,载《中国海洋大学学报》2009 年第 3 期。

陈佳:《新沃尔夫主义概述》,载《外语教学与研究》2011 年第 4 期。

崔希亮:《空间关系的类型学研究》,载《汉语学习》2002 年第 1 期。

储泽祥:《汉语空间短语研究》,北京大学出版社 2010 年版。

董艳萍、桂诗春:《关于双语心理词库的表征结构》,载《外国语》2002 年第 4 期。

桂诗春:《中国学习者英语介词使用概述》,载杨惠中、桂诗春、杨达复编:《基于 CLEC 语料库的中国学习者英语分析》,上海外语教育出版社 2005 年版。

桂诗春、杨惠中:《中国学习者英语语料库》,上海外语教育出版社 2003 年版。

龚嵘、郭秀艳:《双语词汇表征的静态与动态研究视角》,载《外国语》2010 年第 4 期。

姜孟:《语义迁移机制的心理认知研究》,四川大学出版社 2009 年版。

姜孟:《概念迁移:语言迁移研究的新进展》,载《宁夏大学学报》2010 年第 3 期。

孔令达、王祥荣:《儿童语言中方位词的习得及相关问题》,载《中国语文》2002 年第 2 期。

李福印:《认知语言学概论》,北京大学出版社 2008 年版。

李佳、蔡金亭:《认知语言学角度的英语空间介词习得研究》,载《现代外语》2008 年第 2 期。

李俊:《论词汇的深度和广度与阅读理解的关系》,载《外语教学》2003 年第 2 期。

李平:《语言习得的联结主义模式》,载《当代语言学》2002 年第 3 期。

李向农、周国光、孔令达:《1～5 岁儿童运用方位句及方位介词情况的调查分析》,载《心理科学》1992 年第 3 期。

刘振前、石磊:《中国大学生情感、动作隐喻产出对比研究》,载《山东外语教学》2013 年第 6 期。

[英]伦道夫·夸克等:《英语语法大全》,苏州大学《英语语法大全》翻译组译,华东师范大学出版社 1998 年版。

吕叔湘:《现代汉语八百词(增订本)》,商务印书馆 1999 年版。

马书红:《中国学生对英语空间介词语义的习得研究》,载《现代外语》2007 年第 2 期。

马书红:《英语空间介词语义成员的分类与习得》,载《解放军外国语学院学报》2010 年第 4 期。

牛保义:《自主/依存联结——认知语法的一种分析模型》,载《外语与外语教学》2008 年第 1 期(a)。

牛保义:《自主/依存联结:英语轭式搭配的认知研究》,载《四川外语学院学报》2008 年第 2 期(b)。

牛保义:《新自主/依存联结分析模型的建构与应用》,载《现代外语》2011 年第 3 期。

牛保义:《构式语法理论研究》,上海外语教育出版社 2011 年版。

秦洪武、王克非:《基于语料库的翻译语言分析——以 *so... that* 的汉语对应结构为例》,载《现代外语》2004 年第 1 期。

王初明:《解释二语习得:连接论优于普遍语法》,载《外国语》2001 年第 5 期。

王初明:《外语是怎样学会的》,外语教学与研究出版社 2010 年版。

韦晓保:《第二语言习得理论研究的新视角:D-C-C 模式》,载《外语界》2012 年第 6 期。

文秋芳:《应用语言学研究方法与论文写作》,外语教学与研究出版社 2004 年版。

武和平、魏行:《英汉空间方所表达的认知语义分析——以“里”“上”和“*in*”“*on*”为例》,载《解放军外国语学院学报》2007 年第 3 期。

徐富平:《儿童空间词汇习得研究概述》,载《语文研究与创作》2010 年第 14 期。

徐庆利、蔡金亭、刘振前:《语言迁移研究近 20 年的新发展:回顾与思考》,载《外语学刊》2013 年第 1 期。

徐庆利、刘振前、蔡金亭:《参照物范畴化对中国学习者英语空间介词 in 使用的影响》,载《外语教学与研究》2014 年第 5 期。

许子艳:《英语运动事件表达习得与二语水平关系研究》,载《中国外语》2013 年第 5 期。

杨梅:《母语迁移与英语复数名词短语的二语理解和产出》,载《外语教学与研究》2014 年第 1 期。

张会平、刘永兵:《英语介词学习与概念迁移——以常用介词搭配与类联结为例》,载《外语教学与研究》2013 年第 4 期。

张金生、刘云红:《“里”“中”“内”空间意义的认知语言学考察》,载《解放军外国语学院学报》2008 年第 3 期。

张克定:《关于空间关系构式的几个基本问题》,载《山东外语教学》2013 年第 3 期。

张雷、俞理明:《心理类型在中国学生英语习语理解中的作用》,载《现代外语》2011 年第 2 期。